# AI
# Self-Driving Cars
# Headway

### Practical Advances in
### Artificial Intelligence and Machine Learning

## Dr. Lance B. Eliot, MBA, PhD

# DEDICATION

To my incredible daughter, Lauren, and my incredible son, Michael.

*Forest fortuna adiuvat* (from the Latin; good fortune favors the brave).

# CONTENTS

Acknowledgments ...................................................... iii

Introduction ........................................................... 1

**Chapters**

1  Eliot Framework for AI Self-Driving Cars  .............................. 15

2  Germ Spreading and AI Self-Driving Cars .............................. 29

3  Carbon Footprint and AI Self-Driving Cars ........................... 39

4  Protestors Use Of AI Self-Driving Cars ............................. 49

5  Rogue Behavior and AI Self-Driving Cars ...................... 59

6  Using Human Drivers Versus AI Self-Driving Cars ............ 73

7  Tesla Hodge-Podge and AI Self-Driving Cars ...................... 89

8  Solo Occupancy and AI Self-Driving Cars ......................... 101

9  Einstein's Twins Paradox and AI Self-Driving Cars............. 113

10  Nation-State Takeover Of AI Self-Driving Cars ............... 125

11  Quantum Computers and AI Self-Driving Cars .................. 139

12  Religious Revival and AI Self-Driving Cars ......................... 153

Appendix A: Teaching with this Material ......................... 165

Other Self-Driving Car Books by This Author .................. 173

About the Author ..................................................... 245

Addendum ........................................................... 246

Lance B. Eliot

# ACKNOWLEDGMENTS

I have been the beneficiary of advice and counsel by many friends, colleagues, family, investors, and many others. I want to thank everyone that has aided me throughout my career. I write from the heart and the head, having experienced first-hand what it means to have others around you that support you during the good times and the tough times.

To Warren Bennis, one of my doctoral advisors and ultimately a colleague, I offer my deepest thanks and appreciation, especially for his calm and insightful wisdom and support.

To Mark Stevens and his generous efforts toward funding and supporting the USC Stevens Center for Innovation.

To Lloyd Greif and the USC Lloyd Greif Center for Entrepreneurial Studies for their ongoing encouragement of founders and entrepreneurs.

To Peter Drucker, William Wang, Aaron Levie, Peter Kim, Jon Kraft, Cindy Crawford, Jenny Ming, Steve Milligan, Chis Underwood, Frank Gehry, Buzz Aldrin, Steve Forbes, Bill Thompson, Dave Dillon, Alan Fuerstman, Larry Ellison, Jim Sinegal, John Sperling, Mark Stevenson, Anand Nallathambi, Thomas Barrack, Jr., and many other innovators and leaders that I have met and gained mightily from doing so.

Thanks to Ed Trainor, Kevin Anderson, James Hickey, Wendell Jones, Ken Harris, DuWayne Peterson, Mike Brown, Jim Thornton, Abhi Beniwal, Al Biland, John Nomura, Eliot Weinman, John Desmond, and many others for their unwavering support during my career.

*And most of all thanks as always to Lauren and Michael, for their ongoing support and for having seen me writing and heard much of this material during the many months involved in writing it. To their patience and willingness to listen.*

Lance B. Eliot

# INTRODUCTION

This is a book that provides the newest innovations and the latest Artificial Intelligence (AI) advances about the emerging nature of AI-based autonomous self-driving driverless cars. Via recent advances in Artificial Intelligence (AI) and Machine Learning (ML), we are nearing the day when vehicles can control themselves and will not require and nor rely upon human intervention to perform their driving tasks (or, that <u>allow</u> for human intervention, but only *require* human intervention in very limited ways).

Similar to my other related books, which I describe in a moment and list the chapters in the Appendix A of this book, I am particularly focused on those advances that pertain to self-driving cars. The phrase "autonomous vehicles" is often used to refer to any kind of vehicle, whether it is ground-based or in the air or sea, and whether it is a cargo hauling trailer truck or a conventional passenger car. Though the aspects described in this book are certainly applicable to all kinds of autonomous vehicles, I am focused more so here on cars.

Indeed, I am especially known for my role in aiding the advancement of self-driving cars, serving currently as the Executive Director of the Cybernetic AI Self-Driving Cars Institute. In addition to writing software, designing and developing systems and software for self-driving cars, I also speak and write quite a bit about the topic. This book is a collection of some of my more advanced essays. For those of you that might have seen my essays posted elsewhere, I have updated them and integrated them into this book as one handy cohesive package.

You might be interested in companion books that I have written that provide additional key innovations and fundamentals about self-driving cars. Those books are entitled **"Introduction to Driverless Self-Driving Cars," "Advances in AI and Autonomous Vehicles: Cybernetic Self-Driving Cars," "Self-Driving Cars: "The Mother of All AI Projects," "Innovation and Thought Leadership on Self-Driving Driverless Cars," "New Advances in AI Autonomous Driverless Self-Driving Cars," "Autonomous Vehicle Driverless Self-Driving Cars and Artificial Intelligence," "Transformative Artificial Intelligence**

Driverless Self-Driving Cars," "Disruptive Artificial Intelligence and Driverless Self-Driving Cars, and "State-of-the-Art AI Driverless Self-Driving Cars," and "Top Trends in AI Self-Driving Cars," and "AI Innovations and Self-Driving Cars," "Crucial Advances for AI Driverless Cars," "Sociotechnical Insights and AI Driverless Cars," "Pioneering Advances for AI Driverless Cars" and "Leading Edge Trends for AI Driverless Cars," "The Cutting Edge of AI Autonomous Cars" and "The Next Wave of AI Self-Driving Cars" and "Revolutionary Innovations of AI Self-Driving Cars," and "AI Self-Driving Cars Breakthroughs," "Trailblazing Trends for AI Self-Driving Cars," "Ingenious Strides for AI Driverless Cars," "AI Self-Driving Cars Inventiveness," "Visionary Secrets of AI Driverless Cars," "Spearheading AI Self-Driving Cars," "Spurring AI Self-Driving Cars," "Avant-Garde AI Driverless Cars," "AI Self-Driving Cars Evolvement," "AI Driverless Cars Chrysalis," "Boosting AI Autonomous Cars," "AI Self-Driving Cars Trendsetting," "AI Autonomous Cars Forefront, "AI Autonomous Cars Emergence," "AI Autonomous Cars Progress," "AI Self-Driving Cars Prognosis," "AI Self-Driving Cars Momentum," "AI Self-Driving Cars Headway" (they are available on Amazon). Appendix A has a listing of the chapters covered.

For this book, I am going to borrow my introduction from those companion books, since it does a good job of laying out the landscape of self-driving cars and my overall viewpoints on the topic. The remainder of this book is material that does not appear in the companion books.

## INTRODUCTION TO SELF-DRIVING CARS

This is a book about self-driving cars. Someday in the future, we'll all have self-driving cars and this book will perhaps seem antiquated, but right now, we are at the forefront of the self-driving car wave. Daily news bombards us with flashes of new announcements by one car maker or another and leaves the impression that within the next few weeks or maybe months that the self-driving car will be here. A casual non-technical reader would assume from these news flashes that in fact we must be on the cusp of a true self-driving car. Here's a real news flash: We are still quite a distance from having a true self-driving car. It is years to go before we get there.

A true self-driving car is akin to a moonshot. In the same manner that getting us to the moon was an incredible feat, likewise, is achieving a true self-driving car. Anybody that suggests or even brashly states that the true self-driving car is nearly here should be viewed with great skepticism. Indeed, you'll see that I often tend to use the word "hogwash" or "crock" when I assess much of the decidedly *fake news* about self-driving cars.

Indeed, I've been writing a popular blog post about self-driving cars and hitting hard on those that try to wave their hands and pretend that we are on the imminent verge of true self-driving cars. For many years, I've been known as the AI Insider. Besides writing about AI, I also develop AI software. I do what I describe. It also gives me insights into what others that are doing AI are really doing versus what it is said they are doing.

Many faithful readers had asked me to pull together my insightful short essays and put them into another book, which you are now holding.

For those of you that have been reading my essays over the years, this collection not only puts them together into one handy package, I also updated the essays and added new material. For those of you that are new to the topic of self-driving cars and AI, I hope you find these essays approachable and informative. I also tend to have a writing style with a bit of a voice, and so you'll see that I am times have a wry sense of humor and poke at conformity.

As a former professor and founder of an AI research lab, I for many years wrote in the formal language of academic writing. I published in referred journals and served as an editor for several AI journals. This writing here is not of the nature, and I have adopted a different and more informal style for these essays. That being said, I also do mention from time-to-time more rigorous material on AI and encourage you all to dig into those deeper and more formal materials if so interested.

I am also an AI practitioner. This means that I write AI software for a living. Currently, I head-up the Cybernetics Self-Driving Car Institute, where we are developing AI software for self-driving cars. I am excited to also report that my son, also a software engineer, heads-up our Cybernetics Self-Driving Car Lab. What I have helped to start, and for which he is an integral part, ultimately he will carry long into the future after I have retired. My daughter, a marketing whiz, also is integral to our efforts as head of our Marketing group. She too will carry forward the legacy now being formulated.

For those of you that are reading this book and have a penchant for writing code, you might consider taking a look at the open source code available for self-driving cars. This is a handy place to start learning how to develop AI for self-driving cars. There are also many new educational courses spring forth. There is a growing body of those wanting to learn about and develop self-driving cars, and a growing body of colleges, labs, and other avenues by which you can learn about self-driving cars.

This book will provide a foundation of aspects that I think will get you ready for those kinds of more advanced training opportunities. If you've already taken those classes, you'll likely find these essays especially interesting as they offer a perspective that I am betting few other instructors or faculty offered to you. These are challenging essays that ask you to think beyond the conventional about self-driving cars.

# THE MOTHER OF ALL AI PROJECTS

In June 2017, Apple CEO Tim Cook came out and finally admitted that Apple has been working on a self-driving car. As you'll see in my essays, Apple was enmeshed in secrecy about their self-driving car efforts. We have only been able to read the tea leaves and guess at what Apple has been up to. The notion of an iCar has been floating for quite a while, and self-driving engineers and researchers have been signing tight-lipped Non-Disclosure Agreements (NDA's) to work on projects at Apple that were as shrouded in mystery as any military invasion plans might be.

Tim Cook said something that many others in the Artificial Intelligence (AI) field have been saying, namely, the creation of a self-driving car has got to be the mother of all AI projects. In other words, it is in fact a tremendous moonshot for AI. If a self-driving car can be crafted and the AI works as we hope, it means that we have made incredible strides with AI and that therefore it opens many other worlds of potential breakthrough accomplishments that AI can solve.

Is this hyperbole? Am I just trying to make AI seem like a miracle worker and so provide self-aggrandizing statements for those of us writing the AI software for self-driving cars? No, it is not hyperbole. Developing a true self-driving car is really, really, really hard to do. Let me take a moment to explain why. As a side note, I realize that the Apple CEO is known for at times uttering hyperbole, and he had previously said for example that the year 2012 was "the mother of all years," and he had said that the release of iOS 10 was "the mother of all releases" – all of which does suggest he likes to use the handy "mother of" expression. But, I assure you, in terms of true self-driving cars, he has hit the nail on the head. For sure.

When you think about a moonshot and how we got to the moon, there are some identifiable characteristics and those same aspects can be applied to creating a true self-driving car. You'll notice that I keep putting the word "true" in front of the self-driving car expression. I do so because as per my essay about the various levels of self-driving cars, there are some self-driving cars that are only somewhat of a self-driving car. The somewhat versions are ones that require a human driver to be ready to intervene. In my view, that's not a true self-driving car. A true self-driving car is one that requires no human driver intervention at all. It is a car that can entirely undertake via automation the driving task without any human driver needed. This is the essence of what is known as a Level 5 self-driving car. We are currently at the Level 2 and Level 3 mark, and not yet at Level 5.

Getting to the moon involved aspects such as having big stretch goals, incremental progress, experimentation, innovation, and so on. Let's review how this applied to the moonshot of the bygone era, and how it applies to the self-driving car moonshot of today.

### Big Stretch Goal

Trying to take a human and deliver the human to the moon, and bring them back, safely, was an extremely large stretch goal at the time. No one knew whether it could be done. The technology wasn't available yet. The cost was huge. The determination would need to be fierce. Etc. To reach a Level 5 self-driving car is going to be the same. It is a big stretch goal. We can readily get to the Level 3, and we are able to see the Level 4 just up ahead, but a Level 5 is still an unknown as to if it is doable. It should eventually be doable and in the same way that we thought we'd eventually get to the moon, but when it will occur is a different story.

### Incremental Progress

Getting to the moon did not happen overnight in one fell swoop. It took years and years of incremental progress to get there. Likewise for self-driving cars. Google has famously been striving to get to the Level 5, and pretty much been willing to forgo dealing with the intervening levels, but most of the other self-driving car makers are doing the incremental route. Let's get a good Level 2 and a somewhat Level 3 going. Then, let's improve the Level 3 and get a somewhat Level 4 going. Then, let's improve the Level 4 and finally arrive at a Level 5. This seems to be the prevalent way that we are going to achieve the true self-driving car.

### Experimentation

You likely know that there were various experiments involved in perfecting the approach and technology to get to the moon. As per making incremental progress, we first tried to see if we could get a rocket to go into space and safety return, then put a monkey in there, then with a human, then we went all the way to the moon but didn't land, and finally we arrived at the mission that actually landed on the moon. Self-driving cars are the same way. We are doing simulations of self-driving cars. We do testing of self-driving cars on private land under controlled situations. We do testing of self-driving cars on public roadways, often having to meet regulatory requirements including for example having an engineer or equivalent in the car to take over the controls if needed. And so on. Experiments big and small are needed to figure out what works and what doesn't.

### Innovation

There are already some advances in AI that are allowing us to progress toward self-driving cars. We are going to need even more advances. Innovation in all aspects of technology are going to be required to achieve a true self-driving car. By no means do we already have everything in-hand that we need to get there. Expect new inventions and new approaches, new algorithms, etc.

### Setbacks

Most of the pundits are avoiding talking about potential setbacks in the progress toward self-driving cars. Getting to the moon involved many setbacks, some of which you never have heard of and were buried at the time so as to not dampen enthusiasm and funding for getting to the moon. A recurring theme in many of my included essays is that there are going to be setbacks as we try to arrive at a true self-driving car. Take a deep breath and be ready. I just hope the setbacks don't completely stop progress. I am sure that it will cause progress to alter in a manner that we've not yet seen in the self-driving car field. I liken the self-driving car of today to the excitement everyone had for Uber when it first got going. Today, we have a different view of Uber and with each passing day there are more regulations to the ride sharing business and more concerns raised. The darling child only stays a darling until finally that child acts up. It will happen the same with self-driving cars.

## SELF-DRIVING CARS CHALLENGES

But what exactly makes things so hard to have a true self-driving car, you might be asking. You have seen cruise control for years and years. You've lately seen cars that can do parallel parking. You've seen YouTube videos of Tesla drivers that put their hands out the window as their car zooms along the highway, and seen to therefore be in a self-driving car. Aren't we just needing to put a few more sensors onto a car and then we'll have in-hand a true self-driving car? Nope.

Consider for a moment the nature of the driving task. We don't just let anyone at any age drive a car. Worldwide, most countries won't license a driver until the age of 18, though many do allow a learner's permit at the age of 15 or 16. Some suggest that a younger age would be physically too small to reach the controls of the car. Though this might be the case, we could easily adjust the controls to allow for younger aged and thus smaller stature. It's not their physical size that matters. It's their cognitive development that matters.

To drive a car, you need to be able to reason about the car, what the car can and cannot do. You need to know how to operate the car. You need to know about how other cars on the road drive. You need to know what is allowed in driving such as speed limits and driving within marked lanes. You need to be able to react to situations and be able to avoid getting into accidents. You need to ascertain when to hit your brakes, when to steer clear of a pedestrian, and how to keep from ramming that motorcyclist that just cut you off.

Many of us had taken courses on driving. We studied about driving and took driver training. We had to take a test and pass it to be able to drive. The point being that though most adults take the driving task for granted, and we often "mindlessly" drive our cars, there is a significant amount of cognitive effort that goes into driving a car. After a while, it becomes second nature. You don't especially think about how you drive, you just do it. But, if you watch a novice driver, say a teenager learning to drive, you suddenly realize that there is a lot more complexity to it than we seem to realize.

Furthermore, driving is a very serious task. I recall when my daughter and son first learned to drive. They are both very conscientious people. They wanted to make sure that whatever they did, they did well, and that they did not harm anyone. Every day, when you get into a car, it is probably around 4,000 pounds of hefty metal and plastics (about two tons), and it is a lethal weapon. Think about it. You drive down the street in an object that weighs two tons and with the engine it can accelerate and ram into anything you want to hit. The damage a car can inflict is very scary. Both my children were surprised that they were being given the right to maneuver this monster of a beast that could cause tremendous harm entirely by merely letting go of the steering wheel for a moment or taking your eyes off the road.

In fact, in the United States alone there are about 30,000 deaths per year by auto accidents, which is around 100 per day. Given that there are about 263 million cars in the United States, I am actually more amazed that the number of fatalities is not a lot higher. During my morning commute, I look at all the thousands of cars on the freeway around me, and I think that if all of them decided to go zombie and drive in a crazy maniac way, there would be many people dead. Somehow, incredibly, each day, most people drive relatively safely. To me, that's a miracle right there. Getting millions and millions of people to be safe and sane when behind the wheel of a two ton mobile object, it's a feat that we as a society should admire with pride.

So, hopefully you are in agreement that the driving task requires a great deal of cognition. You don't' need to be especially smart to drive a car, and we've done quite a bit to make car driving viable for even the average dolt. There isn't an IQ test that you need to take to drive a car. If you can read and write, and pass a test, you pretty much can legally drive a car. There are of course some that drive a car and are not legally permitted to do so, plus there are private areas such as farms where drivers are young, but for public roadways in the United States, you can be generally of average intelligence (or less) and be able to legally drive.

This though makes it seem like the cognitive effort must not be much. If the cognitive effort was truly hard, wouldn't we only have Einstein's that could drive a car? We have made sure to keep the driving task as simple as we can, by making the controls easy and relatively standardized, and by having roads that are relatively standardized, and so on. It is as though Disneyland has put their Autopia into the real-world, by us all as a society agreeing that roads will be a certain way, and we'll all abide by the various rules of driving.

A modest cognitive task by a human is still something that stymies AI. You certainly know that AI has been able to beat chess players and be good at other kinds of games. This type of narrow cognition is not what car driving is about. Car driving is much wider. It requires knowledge about the world, which a chess playing AI system does not need to know. The cognitive aspects of driving are on the one hand seemingly simple, but at the same time require layer upon layer of knowledge about cars, people, roads, rules, and a myriad of other "common sense" aspects. We don't have any AI systems today that have that same kind of breadth and depth of awareness and knowledge.

As revealed in my essays, the self-driving car of today is using trickery to do particular tasks. It is all very narrow in operation. Plus, it currently assumes that a human driver is ready to intervene. It is like a child that we have taught to stack blocks, but we are needed to be right there in case the child stacks them too high and they begin to fall over. AI of today is brittle, it is narrow, and it does not approach the cognitive abilities of humans. This is why the true self-driving car is somewhere out in the future.

Another aspect to the driving task is that it is not solely a mind exercise. You do need to use your senses to drive. You use your eyes a vision sensors to see the road ahead. You vision capability is like a streaming video, which your brain needs to continually analyze as you drive. Where is the road? Is there a pedestrian in the way? Is there another car ahead of you? Your senses are relying a flood of info to your brain. Self-driving cars are trying to do the same, by using cameras, radar, ultrasound, and lasers. This is an attempt at mimicking how humans have senses and sensory apparatus.

Thus, the driving task is mental and physical. You use your senses, you use your arms and legs to manipulate the controls of the car, and you use your brain to assess the sensory info and direct your limbs to act upon the controls of the car. This all happens instantly. If you've ever perhaps gotten something in your eye and only had one eye available to drive with, you suddenly realize how dependent upon vision you are. If you have a broken foot with a cast, you suddenly realize how hard it is to control the brake pedal and the accelerator. If you've taken medication and your brain is maybe sluggish, you suddenly realize how much mental strain is required to drive a car.

An AI system that plays chess only needs to be focused on playing chess. The physical aspects aren't important because usually a human moves the chess pieces or the chessboard is shown on an electronic display. Using AI for a more life-and-death task such as analyzing MRI images of patients, this again does not require physical capabilities and instead is done by examining images of bits.

Driving a car is a true life-and-death task. It is a use of AI that can easily and at any moment produce death. For those colleagues of mine that are developing this AI, as am I, we need to keep in mind the somber aspects of this. We are producing software that will have in its virtual hands the lives of the occupants of the car, and the lives of those in other nearby cars, and the lives of nearby pedestrians, etc. Chess is not usually a life-or-death matter.

Driving is all around us. Cars are everywhere. Most of today's AI applications involve only a small number of people. Or, they are behind the scenes and we as humans have other recourse if the AI messes up. AI that is driving a car at 80 miles per hour on a highway had better not mess up. The consequences are grave. Multiply this by the number of cars, if we could put magically self-driving into every car in the USA, we'd have AI running in the 263 million cars. That's a lot of AI spread around. This is AI on a massive scale that we are not doing today and that offers both promise and potential peril.

There are some that want AI for self-driving cars because they envision a world without any car accidents. They envision a world in which there is no car congestion and all cars cooperate with each other. These are wonderful utopian visions.

They are also very misleading. The adoption of self-driving cars is going to be incremental and not overnight. We cannot economically just junk all existing cars. Nor are we going to be able to affordably retrofit existing cars. It is more likely that self-driving cars will be built into new cars and that over many years of gradual replacement of existing cars that we'll see the mix of self-driving cars become substantial in the real-world.

In these essays, I have tried to offer technological insights without being overly technical in my description, and also blended the business, societal, and economic aspects too. Technologists need to consider the non-technological impacts of what they do. Non-technologists should be aware of what is being developed.

We all need to work together to collectively be prepared for the enormous disruption and transformative aspects of true self-driving cars. We all need to be involved in this mother of all AI projects.

# WHAT THIS BOOK PROVIDES

What does this book provide to you? It introduces many of the key elements about self-driving cars and does so with an AI based perspective. I weave together technical and non-technical aspects, readily going from being concerned about the cognitive capabilities of the driving task and how the technology is embodying this into self-driving cars, and in the next breath I discuss the societal and economic aspects.

They are all intertwined because that's the way reality is. You cannot separate out the technology per se, and instead must consider it within the milieu of what is being invented and innovated, and do so with a mindset towards the contemporary mores and culture that shape what we are doing and what we hope to do.

# WHY THIS BOOK

I wrote this book to try and bring to the public view many aspects about self-driving cars that nobody seems to be discussing.

For business leaders that are either involved in making self-driving cars or that are going to leverage self-driving cars, I hope that this book will enlighten you as to the risks involved and ways in which you should be strategizing about how to deal with those risks.

For entrepreneurs, startups and other businesses that want to enter into the self-driving car market that is emerging, I hope this book sparks your interest in doing so, and provides some sense of what might be prudent to pursue.

For researchers that study self-driving cars, I hope this book spurs your interest in the risks and safety issues of self-driving cars, and also nudges you toward conducting research on those aspects.

For students in computer science or related disciplines, I hope this book will provide you with interesting and new ideas and material, for which you might conduct research or provide some career direction insights for you.

For AI companies and high-tech companies pursuing self-driving cars, this book will hopefully broaden your view beyond just the mere coding and development needed to make self-driving cars.

For all readers, I hope that you will find the material in this book to be stimulating. Some of it will be repetitive of things you already know. But I am pretty sure that you'll also find various eureka moments whereby you'll discover a new technique or approach that you had not earlier thought of. I am also betting that there will be material that forces you to rethink some of your current practices.

I am not saying you will suddenly have an epiphany and change what you are doing. I do think though that you will reconsider or perhaps revisit what you are doing.

For anyone choosing to use this book for teaching purposes, please take a look at my suggestions for doing so, as described in the Appendix. I have found the material handy in courses that I have taught, and likewise other faculty have told me that they have found the material handy, in some cases as extended readings and in other instances as a core part of their course (depending on the nature of the class).

In my writing for this book, I have tried carefully to blend both the practitioner and the academic styles of writing. It is not as dense as is typical academic journal writing, but at the same time offers depth by going into the nuances and trade-offs of various practices.

The word "deep" is in vogue today, meaning getting deeply into a subject or topic, and so is the word "unpack" which means to tease out the underlying aspects of a subject or topic. I have sought to offer material that addresses an issue or topic by going relatively deeply into it and make sure that it is well unpacked.

In any book about AI, it is difficult to use our everyday words without having some of them be misinterpreted. Specifically, it is easy to anthropomorphize AI. When I say that an AI system "knows" something, I do not want you to construe that the AI system has sentience and "knows" in the same way that humans do. They aren't that way, as yet. I have tried to use quotes around such words from time-to-time to emphasize that the words I am using should not be misinterpreted to ascribe true human intelligence to the AI systems that we know of today. If I used quotes around all such words, the book would be very difficult to read, and so I am doing so judiciously. Please keep that in mind as you read the material, thanks.

Some of the material is time-based in terms of covering underway activities, and though some of it might decay, nonetheless I believe you'll find the material useful and informative.

# COMPANION BOOKS

1. **"Introduction to Driverless Self-Driving Cars"** by Dr. Lance Eliot
2. **"Innovation and Thought Leadership on Self-Driving Driverless Cars"** by Dr. Lance Eliot
3. **"Advances in AI and Autonomous Vehicles: Cybernetic Self-Driving Cars"** by Dr. Lance Eliot
4. **"Self-Driving Cars: The Mother of All AI Projects"** by Dr. Lance Eliot
5. **"New Advances in AI Autonomous Driverless Self-Driving Cars"** by Dr. Lance Eliot
6. **"Autonomous Vehicle Driverless Self-Driving Cars and Artificial Intelligence"** by Dr. Lance Eliot and Michael B. Eliot
7. **"Transformative Artificial Intelligence Driverless Self-Driving Cars"** by Dr. Lance Eliot
8. **"Disruptive Artificial Intelligence and Driverless Self-Driving Cars"** by Dr. Lance Eliot
9. "State-of-the-Art AI Driverless Self-Driving Cars" by Dr. Lance Eliot
10. "Top Trends in AI Self-Driving Cars" by Dr. Lance Eliot
11. **"AI Innovations and Self-Driving Cars"** by Dr. Lance Eliot
12. **"Crucial Advances for AI Driverless Cars"** by Dr. Lance Eliot
13. **"Sociotechnical Insights and AI Driverless Cars"** by Dr. Lance Eliot.
14. **"Pioneering Advances for AI Driverless Cars"** by Dr. Lance Eliot
15. **"Leading Edge Trends for AI Driverless Cars"** by Dr. Lance Eliot
16. **"The Cutting Edge of AI Autonomous Cars"** by Dr. Lance Eliot
17. **"The Next Wave of AI Self-Driving Cars"** by Dr. Lance Eliot
18. **"Revolutionary Innovations of AI Driverless Cars"** by Dr. Lance Eliot
19. **"AI Self-Driving Cars Breakthroughs"** by Dr. Lance Eliot
20. **"Trailblazing Trends for AI Self-Driving Cars"** by Dr. Lance Eliot
21. **"Ingenious Strides for AI Driverless Cars"** by Dr. Lance Eliot
22. **"AI Self-Driving Cars Inventiveness"** by Dr. Lance Eliot
23. **"Visionary Secrets of AI Driverless Cars"** by Dr. Lance Eliot
24. **"Spearheading AI Self-Driving Cars"** by Dr. Lance Eliot
25. **"Spurring AI Self-Driving Cars"** by Dr. Lance Eliot
26. **"Avant-Garde AI Driverless Cars"** by Dr. Lance Eliot
27. **"AI Self-Driving Cars Evolvement"** by Dr. Lance Eliot
28. **"AI Driverless Cars Chrysalis"** by Dr. Lance Eliot
29. **"Boosting AI Autonomous Cars"** by Dr. Lance Eliot
30. **"AI Self-Driving Cars Trendsetting"** by Dr. Lance Eliot
31. **"AI Autonomous Cars Forefront"** by Dr. Lance Eliot
32. **"AI Autonomous Cars Emergence"** by Dr. Lance Eliot
33. **"AI Autonomous Cars Progress"** by Dr. Lance Eliot
34. **"AI Self-Driving Cars Prognosis"** by Dr. Lance Eliot
35. **"AI Self-Driving Cars Momentum"** by Dr. Lance Eliot
36. **"AI Self-Driving Cars Headway"** by Dr. Lance Eliot

These books are available on Amazon and at other major global booksellers.

# CHAPTER 1

# ELIOT FRAMEWORK FOR AI SELF-DRIVING CARS

# CHAPTER 1

# ELIOT FRAMEWORK FOR AI SELF-DRIVING CARS

This chapter is a core foundational aspect for understanding AI self-driving cars and I have used this same chapter in several of my other books to introduce the reader to essential elements of this field. Once you've read this chapter, you'll be prepared to read the rest of the material since the foundational essence of the components of autonomous AI driverless self-driving cars will have been established for you.

––––––––––

When I give presentations about self-driving cars and teach classes on the topic, I have found it helpful to provide a framework around which the various key elements of self-driving cars can be understood and organized (see diagram at the end of this chapter). The framework needs to be simple enough to convey the overarching elements, but at the same time not so simple that it belies the true complexity of self-driving cars. As such, I am going to describe the framework here and try to offer in a thousand words (or more!) what the framework diagram itself intends to portray.

The core elements on the diagram are numbered for ease of reference. The numbering does not suggest any kind of prioritization of the elements. Each element is crucial. Each element has a purpose, and otherwise would not be included in the framework. For some self-driving cars, a particular element might be more important or somehow distinguished in comparison to other self-driving cars.

You could even use the framework to rate a particular self-driving car, doing so by gauging how well it performs in each of the elements of the framework. I will describe each of the elements, one at a time. After doing so, I'll discuss aspects that illustrate how the elements interact and perform during the overall effort of a self-driving car.

At the Cybernetic Self-Driving Car Institute, we use the framework to keep track of what we are working on, and how we are developing software that fills in what is needed to achieve Level 5 self-driving cars.

### D-01: Sensor Capture

Let's start with the one element that often gets the most attention in the press about self-driving cars, namely, the sensory devices for a self-driving car.

On the framework, the box labeled as D-01 indicates "Sensor Capture" and refers to the processes of the self-driving car that involve collecting data from the myriad of sensors that are used for a self-driving car. The types of devices typically involved are listed, such as the use of mono cameras, stereo cameras, LIDAR devices, radar systems, ultrasonic devices, GPS, IMU, and so on.

These devices are tasked with obtaining data about the status of the self-driving car and the world around it. Some of the devices are continually providing updates, while others of the devices await an indication by the self-driving car that the device is supposed to collect data. The data might be first transformed in some fashion by the device itself, or it might instead be fed directly into the sensor capture as raw data. At that point, it might be up to the sensor capture processes to do transformations on the data. This all varies depending upon the nature of the devices being used and how the devices were designed and developed.

### D-02: Sensor Fusion

Imagine that your eyeballs receive visual images, your nose receives odors, your ears receive sounds, and in essence each of your distinct sensory devices is getting some form of input. The input befits the nature of the device. Likewise, for a self-driving car, the cameras provide visual images, the radar returns radar reflections, and so on.

Each device provides the data as befits what the device does.

At some point, using the analogy to humans, you need to merge together what your eyes see, what your nose smells, what your ears hear, and piece it all together into a larger sense of what the world is all about and what is happening around you. Sensor fusion is the action of taking the singular aspects from each of the devices and putting them together into a larger puzzle.

Sensor fusion is a tough task. There are some devices that might not be working at the time of the sensor capture. Or, there might some devices that are unable to report well what they have detected. Again, using a human analogy, suppose you are in a dark room and so your eyes cannot see much. At that point, you might need to rely more so on your ears and what you hear. The same is true for a self-driving car. If the cameras are obscured due to snow and sleet, it might be that the radar can provide a greater indication of what the external conditions consist of.

In the case of a self-driving car, there can be a plethora of such sensory devices. Each is reporting what it can. Each might have its difficulties. Each might have its limitations, such as how far ahead it can detect an object. All of these limitations need to be considered during the sensor fusion task.

D-03: Virtual World Model

For humans, we presumably keep in our minds a model of the world around us when we are driving a car. In your mind, you know that the car is going at say 60 miles per hour and that you are on a freeway. You have a model in your mind that your car is surrounded by other cars, and that there are lanes to the freeway. Your model is not only based on what you can see, hear, etc., but also what you know about the nature of the world. You know that at any moment that car ahead of you can smash on its brakes, or the car behind you can ram into your car, or that the truck in the next lane might swerve into your lane.

The AI of the self-driving car needs to have a virtual world model, which it then keeps updated with whatever it is receiving from the sensor fusion, which received its input from the sensor capture and the sensory devices.

D-04: System Action Plan

By having a virtual world model, the AI of the self-driving car is able to keep track of where the car is and what is happening around the car. In addition, the AI needs to determine what to do next. Should the self-driving car hit its brakes? Should the self-driving car stay in its lane or swerve into the lane to the left? Should the self-driving car accelerate or slow down?

A system action plan needs to be prepared by the AI of the self-driving car. The action plan specifies what actions should be taken. The actions need to pertain to the status of the virtual world model. Plus, the actions need to be realizable.

This realizability means that the AI cannot just assert that the self-driving car should suddenly sprout wings and fly. Instead, the AI must be bound by whatever the self-driving car can actually do, such as coming to a halt in a distance of X feet at a speed of Y miles per hour, rather than perhaps asserting that the self-driving car come to a halt in 0 feet as though it could instantaneously come to a stop while it is in motion.

D-05: Controls Activation

The system action plan is implemented by activating the controls of the car to act according to what the plan stipulates. This might mean that the accelerator control is commanded to increase the speed of the car. Or, the steering control is commanded to turn the steering wheel 30 degrees to the left or right.

One question arises as to whether or not the controls respond as they are commanded to do. In other words, suppose the AI has commanded the accelerator to increase, but for some reason it does not do so. Or, maybe it tries to do so, but the speed of the car does not increase. The controls activation feeds back into the virtual world model, and simultaneously the virtual world model is getting updated from the sensors, the sensor capture, and the sensor fusion. This allows the AI to ascertain what has taken place as a result of the controls being commanded to take some kind of action.

By the way, please keep in mind that though the diagram seems to have a linear progression to it, the reality is that these are all aspects of the self-driving car that are happening in parallel and simultaneously. The sensors are capturing data, meanwhile the sensor fusion is taking place, meanwhile the virtual model is being updated, meanwhile the system action plan is being formulated and reformulated, meanwhile the controls are being activated.

This is the same as a human being that is driving a car. They are eyeballing the road, meanwhile they are fusing in their mind the sights, sounds, etc., meanwhile their mind is updating their model of the world around them, meanwhile they are formulating an action plan of what to do, and meanwhile they are pushing their foot onto the pedals and steering the car. In the normal course of driving a car, you are doing all of these at once. I mention this so that when you look at the diagram, you will think of the boxes as processes that are all happening at the same time, and not as though only one happens and then the next.

They are shown diagrammatically in a simplistic manner to help comprehend what is taking place. You though should also realize that they are working in parallel and simultaneous with each other. This is a tough aspect in that the inter-element communications involve latency and other aspects that must be taken into account. There can be delays in one element updating and then sharing its latest status with other elements.

D-06: Automobile & CAN

Contemporary cars use various automotive electronics and a Controller Area Network (CAN) to serve as the components that underlie the driving aspects of a car. There are Electronic Control Units (ECU's) which control subsystems of the car, such as the engine, the brakes, the doors, the windows, and so on.

The elements D-01, D-02, D-03, D-04, D-05 are layered on top of the D-06, and must be aware of the nature of what the D-06 is able to do and not do.

D-07: In-Car Commands

Humans are going to be occupants in self-driving cars. In a Level 5 self-driving car, there must be some form of communication that takes place between the humans and the self-driving car. For example, I go into a self-driving car and tell it that I want to be driven over to Disneyland, and along the way I want to stop at In-and-Out Burger. The self-driving car now parses what I've said and tries to then establish a means to carry out my wishes.

In-car commands can happen at any time during a driving journey. Though my example was about an in-car command when I first got into my self-driving car, it could be that while the self-driving car is carrying out the journey that I change my mind. Perhaps after getting stuck in traffic, I tell the self-driving car to forget about getting the burgers and just head straight over to the theme park. The self-driving car needs to be alert to in-car commands throughout the journey.

### D-08: V2X Communications

We will ultimately have self-driving cars communicating with each other, doing so via V2V (Vehicle-to-Vehicle) communications. We will also have self-driving cars that communicate with the roadways and other aspects of the transportation infrastructure, doing so via V2I (Vehicle-to-Infrastructure).

The variety of ways in which a self-driving car will be communicating with other cars and infrastructure is being called V2X, whereby the letter X means whatever else we identify as something that a car should or would want to communicate with. The V2X communications will be taking place simultaneous with everything else on the diagram, and those other elements will need to incorporate whatever it gleans from those V2X communications.

### D-09: Deep Learning

The use of Deep Learning permeates all other aspects of the self-driving car. The AI of the self-driving car will be using deep learning to do a better job at the systems action plan, and at the controls activation, and at the sensor fusion, and so on.

Currently, the use of artificial neural networks is the most prevalent form of deep learning. Based on large swaths of data, the neural networks attempt to "learn" from the data and therefore direct the efforts of the self-driving car accordingly.

D-10: Tactical AI

Tactical AI is the element of dealing with the moment-to-moment driving of the self-driving car. Is the self-driving car staying in its lane of the freeway? Is the car responding appropriately to the controls commands? Are the sensory devices working?

For human drivers, the tactical equivalent can be seen when you watch a novice driver such as a teenager that is first driving. They are focused on the mechanics of the driving task, keeping their eye on the road while also trying to properly control the car.

D-11: Strategic AI

The Strategic AI aspects of a self-driving car are dealing with the larger picture of what the self-driving car is trying to do. If I had asked that the self-driving car take me to Disneyland, there is an overall journey map that needs to be kept and maintained.

There is an interaction between the Strategic AI and the Tactical AI. The Strategic AI is wanting to keep on the mission of the driving, while the Tactical AI is focused on the particulars underway in the driving effort. If the Tactical AI seems to wander away from the overarching mission, the Strategic AI wants to see why and get things back on track. If the Tactical AI realizes that there is something amiss on the self-driving car, it needs to alert the Strategic AI accordingly and have an adjustment to the overarching mission that is underway.

D-12: Self-Aware AI

Very few of the self-driving cars being developed are including a Self-Aware AI element, which we at the Cybernetic Self-Driving Car Institute believe is crucial to Level 5 self-driving cars.

The Self-Aware AI element is intended to watch over itself, in the sense that the AI is making sure that the AI is working as intended. Suppose you had a human driving a car, and they were starting to drive erratically. Hopefully, their own self-awareness would make them realize they themselves are driving poorly, such as perhaps starting to fall asleep after having been driving for hours on end. If you had a passenger in the car, they might be able to alert the driver if the driver is starting to do something amiss. This is exactly what the Self-Aware

AI element tries to do, it becomes the overseer of the AI, and tries to detect when the AI has become faulty or confused, and then find ways to overcome the issue.

### D-13: Economic

The economic aspects of a self-driving car are not per se a technology aspect of a self-driving car, but the economics do indeed impact the nature of a self-driving car. For example, the cost of outfitting a self-driving car with every kind of possible sensory device is prohibitive, and so choices need to be made about which devices are used. And, for those sensory devices chosen, whether they would have a full set of features or a more limited set of features.

We are going to have self-driving cars that are at the low-end of a consumer cost point, and others at the high-end of a consumer cost point. You cannot expect that the self-driving car at the low-end is going to be as robust as the one at the high-end. I realize that many of the self-driving car pundits are acting as though all self-driving cars will be the same, but they won't be. Just like anything else, we are going to have self-driving cars that have a range of capabilities. Some will be better than others. Some will be safer than others. This is the way of the real-world, and so we need to be thinking about the economics aspects when considering the nature of self-driving cars.

### D-14: Societal

This component encompasses the societal aspects of AI which also impacts the technology of self-driving cars. For example, the famous Trolley Problem involves what choices should a self-driving car make when faced with life-and-death matters. If the self-driving car is about to either hit a child standing in the roadway, or instead ram into a tree at the side of the road and possibly kill the humans in the self-driving car, which choice should be made?

We need to keep in mind the societal aspects will underlie the AI of the self-driving car. Whether we are aware of it explicitly or not, the AI will have embedded into it various societal assumptions.

D-15: Innovation

I included the notion of innovation into the framework because we can anticipate that whatever a self-driving car consists of, it will continue to be innovated over time. The self-driving cars coming out in the next several years will undoubtedly be different and less innovative than the versions that come out in ten years hence, and so on.

Framework Overall

For those of you that want to learn about self-driving cars, you can potentially pick a particular element and become specialized in that aspect. Some engineers are focusing on the sensory devices. Some engineers focus on the controls activation. And so on. There are specialties in each of the elements.

Researchers are likewise specializing in various aspects. For example, there are researchers that are using Deep Learning to see how best it can be used for sensor fusion. There are other researchers that are using Deep Learning to derive good System Action Plans. Some are studying how to develop AI for the Strategic aspects of the driving task, while others are focused on the Tactical aspects.

A well-prepared all-around software developer that is involved in self-driving cars should be familiar with all of the elements, at least to the degree that they know what each element does. This is important since whatever piece of the pie that the software developer works on, they need to be knowledgeable about what the other elements are doing.

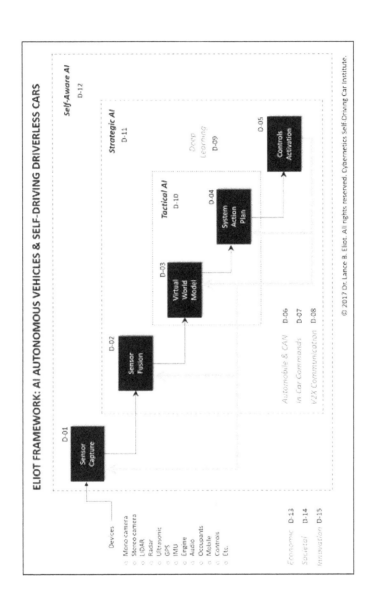

ELIOT FRAMEWORK: AI AUTONOMOUS VEHICLES & SELF-DRIVING DRIVERLESS CARS

Self-Aware AI
D-12

Strategic AI
D-11

Deep
Learning
D-09

Tactical AI
D-10

Sensor
Capture
D-01

Sensor
Fusion
D-02

Virtual
World
Model
D-03

System
Action
Plan
D-04

Controls
Activation
D-05

Devices
○ Mono camera
○ Stereo camera
○ LIDAR
○ Radar
○ Ultrasonic
○ GPS
○ IMU
○ Engine
○ Audio
○ Occupants
○ Mobile
○ Controls
○ Etc.

Automobile & CAN    D-06
In Car Commands     D-07
V2X Communication   D-08

Economic      D-13
Societal      D-14
Innovation    D-15

# CHAPTER 2
# GERM SPREADING
# AND
# AI SELF-DRIVING CARS

# CHAPTER 2

# GERM SPREADING
# AND AI SELF-DRIVING CARS

Germs are all around us, but they might be found in places that you didn't particularly think they were lurking.

Are there germs on a toilet seat? Sure, we all know that.

Here's what might surprise you, there are apparently more germs on the backseat of today's human-driven ridesharing cars than the volume of germs found on toilet seats (according to a recent study by an insurance firm).

The next time you get into a conventional ridesharing car, perhaps eye that backseat with some dismay and disdain, and make sure you sit down cautiously and keep your hands away from the grimy surface.

We probably should be a bit cautious in over-generalizing the research study since it only included nine vehicles consisting of three randomly selected ridesharing cars, along with three randomly selected taxis and three randomly selected rental cars. Researchers used swabs to collect samples of what existed on the surfaces of the backseats and some other areas within the subject cars. The primary metric used to analyze the swabs was the number of colony-forming units, known as CFU's, per square inch, and a subsequent examination of the proportions of different germs types, such as bacillus, cocci, yeast, and other elements.

I'm sure that you already know that various amounts of bacillus germs can possibly cause you to become infected and suffer accordingly, and that exposure to quantities of cocci can lead to pneumonia and blood poisoning. It's a scary germ infecting world that we live in.

These germs don't necessarily magically attack you, instead you typically have to help them get inroads into your body, such as touching the germs with your hands and then putting your fingers into or onto your mouth or nostrils. In one sense, your body is like a castle that tries to keep germs at bay, and meanwhile you can unknowingly let them in via an open castle window or other passageway.

According to these germ seeking scientists with their swabs, they discovered that ridesharing car backseats had more germs than do toilet seats (well, in comparison to the average everyday toilet seat, which maybe you keep yours exactingly cleaner at home), and they also revealed that ridesharing was the worst germ-monger over rental cars, and that taxis were the lesser of the three in terms of harboring nasty germs.

Why would ridesharing cars be the worse of the three?

The most likely answer seems to be that rental cars and taxis tend to get regularly cleaned, frequently occurring at the end of a shift or the end of the day.

There is normally a standard operating procedure (SOP) for rental agencies that entails them cleaning the interior of rented cars upon return. For cabs, usually the cab agency will do a wipe-down on a regular schedule. Before you yell at me that you've been in many cabs that were filthy, and rented rental cars that seemed like they hadn't been cleaned in a year, yes, I realize that does occur, but presumably, on the balance, there is a greater chance that a cab or rental car might get regular cleaning versus a ridesharing car.

Most ridesharing cars are owned and operated by an individual serving as the ridesharing driver. They might not have any regular schedule they observe to clean the interior of their vehicle. Of course, if they pick-up someone from a late-night bar and the person upchucks in the backseat, hopefully a thorough cleaning will be instigated. Overall, and without offending ridesharing drivers, the odds are they aren't cleaning their backseat with any regular pattern (okay, there are exceptions, and I've been in ridesharing cars that you could eat off the backseat without much concern).

My point in bringing this germ foreboding news is that it can give us a heads-up about something that might well occur in the future, namely, it could be that once we have self-driving driverless cars the backseats of those autonomous cars might be as bad or even worse than today's ridesharing germ-mobiles.

Let me explain why.

## Autonomous Cars As Non-Stop Ridesharing Transportation

It is widely assumed that once we have autonomous cars available there will be a tremendous surge in ridesharing and mobility, some saying that we are going to become a mobility-based economy. Whereas today you need to find a car that perchance has available a human driver, in the future there won't presumably be any delay or difficulty about finding a driver since the autonomous car has its own built-in AI driving capability.

Thus, you can summon an autonomous car at your whim and be whisked away.

In fact, it is further anticipated that autonomous cars will be running essentially non-stop, 24x7, seven days a week, week upon week. This is partially due to the idea that there is no driver that needs any resting, and also under the belief that the way to recoup the costs associated with owning a self-driving car will be to rent it out as much as possible.

That being said, admittedly we need to be realistic and include into this equation that a car is still a car, meaning that even autonomous cars will need some amount of "downtime" for purposes of maintenance, repairs, and the like (plus, there's the time needed to refuel or recharge), but I'd bet that the owner of an autonomous car will aim to minimize that non-money-making downtime.

Suppose that today's ridesharing cars are getting maybe 8 hours of use per day, possibly less or more depending upon the ridesharing driver and whether they are working full-time or part-time at providing a ridesharing service. If those ridesharing cars are getting a dose of accumulated germs, you need to ponder what the germs level will be inside an autonomous car that is working around-the-clock.

It seems relatively reasonable to anticipate that the germ counts will go up and that an autonomous car being used for ridesharing has the potential to be a veritable germ factory.

I know that some might think this is all nonsense kind of talk and hyperbole about germs. I would not be so fast to let this matter get filed under the nonsensical category. There would be a heightened chance that with more people using cars, and with the boosted time of collecting germs, things could get out-of-hand. The driverless car would be a ready means of transporting and transferring germs across a wide swath of people in a relatively short period of time.

Kind of like a futuristic virus carrier that's primed to inadvertently spread infection.

Fortunately, since we can predict the scourge, there's a good chance to prevent it from occurring or at least try to mitigate the odds of it getting out-of-control.

## Solving The Autonomous Car Germ Infecting Dangers

There is a slew of ways to overcome the germ raging aspects of autonomous cars. Hopefully, some or all of these approaches that I mention herein will be put into practice once autonomous cars become prevalent.

By the way, the public roadway tryouts of driverless cars are rather minimal today, plus those self-driving cars are being doted over by a dedicated technician crew, so I'd wager that today's autonomous cars aren't prone to the same germ craze as what will happen once we have them all about us. I say this because if you get into an autonomous car today, presumably it's going to have a cleaner backseat than the typical ridesharing car and likely even better than an everyday rental car or a cab.

Here's some solutions or remedies to consider about germ-stopping a future germ-spreading autonomous car world:

- Whenever the autonomous car is getting its ongoing maintenance, the interior should get a proper scrubbing and cleaning. Though this does mean that the amount of downtime will get extended, it could not only help the health of us all, it could also be a marketing point that would attract passengers to use your autonomous car over others that maybe aren't being as clean-minded.

- Provide hand sanitizer in the autonomous car for use by passengers. This adds some cost, I realize, and you'd need to make sure the soap is being replenished, but once again this has both a positive health impact and can be another handy marketing pitch.

- Use an anti-microbial treatment on the interior surfaces of the autonomous car. Similar to how fitness equipment in gyms are increasing applying anti-microbial treatments, this could be a more maintenance-free (or less maintenance) way to try and mitigate germ spreading.

- Consider using electrostatic technology that would be embedded into the autonomous car. The idea of electrostatic tech is that you apply a charge to a surface, and it zaps the germs dead. This might be something that could be incorporated into the interior of a driverless car, though it would be important to obviously only allow the usage of it when safe to do so (watch out for the AI decided to deploy it on unruly passengers!).

- Ask passengers of the driverless car to voluntarily do cleaning while inside for a journey, or possibly offer a discount on the fare for doing so. This is a somewhat debatable approach and it would be hard to know whether people will favor this, and if they do it won't be so easily controlled. Though, since it is assumed that autonomous cars are likely to have cameras pointing inward, doing so to detect when passengers try to rip apart your ridesharing driverless car, it could possibly also showcase whether a passenger really did some cleaning or not.

## Conclusion

I'm guessing that the germs issue concerning autonomous cars won't dawn on anyone until we end-up in the middle of it.

Once autonomous cars are prevalent, there will undoubtedly by some kind of breakout of an infection, and it will be traced to having originated via transfer of germs within a driverless car. At that time, there will be a tremendous public outcry, and perhaps regulators that rush to push forward legislation about keeping the interiors of driverless cars germ-free.

As such, you don't have to right now lay awake at night worrying about autonomous cars and their germ spreading proclivities. I'd suggest instead you be thinking about your next ridesharing trip and bring with you an array of cleaning products for a safer ride.

# CHAPTER 3
# CARBON FOOTPRINT
# AND
# AI SELF-DRIVING CARS

# CHAPTER 3

# CARBON FOOTPRINT
# AND
# AI SELF-DRIVING CARS

The news constantly reminds us about the carbon footprint (CFP) that we are producing.

In some cases, the carbon footprint is expressed for particular modes of transportation such as the amount of carbon dioxide emissions when you fly in a commercial plane from Los Angeles to New York, or when you drive your gasoline powered car from Silicon Valley to Silicon Beach.

Carbon accounting is used to figure out how much a machine or system produces in terms of its carbon footprint when being utilized, and can be calculated for planes, cars, washing machines, refrigerators, and just about anything that emits carbon fumes.

We all seem to now know that our cars are emitting various greenhouses gasses including the dreaded carbon dioxide vapors that have numerous adverse environmental impacts. Some are quick to point out that hybrid cars that use both gasoline and electrical power tend to have a lower carbon footprint than conventional cars, while Electrical Vehicles (EV's) are essentially zero carbon emissions at the tailpipe.

## Calculating Carbon Footprints For A Car

When ascertaining the carbon footprint of a machine or device, it is easy to fall into the mental trap of only considering the emissions that occur when the apparatus is in-use. A gasoline car might emit 200 grams of carbon dioxide per kilometer traveled, while a hybrid-electric might produce about half at 92 grams, and an EV presumably at 0 grams, per EPA and Department of Energy estimates.

Though the direct carbon footprint aspect does indeed involve what happens during the utilization effort of a machine or device, there is also the indirect carbon footprint that requires our equal attention, involving both upstream and downstream elements that contribute to a fuller picture of the true carbon footprint involved. For example, a conventional gasoline powered car might generate perhaps 28 percent of its total life-time carbon dioxide emissions when the car was originally manufactured and shipped to being sold.

You might at first be normally thinking like this:

- Total CFP of a car = CFP while burning gasoline

But it should be more like this:

- Total CFP of a car = CFP when car is made + CFP while burning gasoline

Let's define "CFP Made" as a factor about the carbon footprint when a car is manufactured and shipped, and another factor we'll call "CFP FuelUse" that represents the carbon footprint while the car is operating.

For the full lifecycle of a car, we actually need to add more factors into the equation.

There is a carbon footprint when the gasoline itself is being generated, I'll call it "CFP FuelGen," and thus we should include not just the CFP when the fuel is consumed but also when the fuel was originally processed or generated. Furthermore, once a car has seen its day and will be put aside and no longer used, there is a carbon footprint associate with disposing or scrapping of the car ("CFP Disposal").

This also brings up a facet about EV's. The attention of EV's as having zero CFP at the tailpipe is somewhat misleading when considering the total lifecycle CFP, since you should also be including the carbon footprint required to generate the electrical power that gets charged into the EV and then is consumed while the EV is driving around. We'll assign that amount into the CFP FuelGen factor.

The expanded formula is:

- Total CFP of a car = CFP Made + CFP FuelUse + CFP FuelGen + CFP Disposal

Let's rearrange the factors to group together the one-time carbon footprint amounts, which would be the CFP Made and CFP Disposal, and group together the ongoing usage carbon footprint amounts, which would be the CFP FuelUse and CFP FuelGen. This makes sense since the fuel used and the fuel generated factors are going to vary depending upon how much a particular car is actually being driven. Presumably, a low mileage driven car that mainly sits in your garage would have a smaller grand-total over its lifetime of the CFP consumption amount than would a car that's being driven all the time and racking up tons of miles.

The rearranged overall formula is:

- Total CFP of a car = (CFP Made + CFP Disposal) + (CFP FuelUse + CFP FuelGen)

*Next, I'd like to add a twist that very few are considering when it comes to the emergence of self-driving autonomous cars, namely the carbon footprint associated with the AI Machine Learning for driverless cars.*

Let's call that amount as "CFP ML" and add it into the equation.

- Total CFP of a car = (CFP Made + CFP Disposal) + (CFP FuelUse + CFP FuelGen) + CFP ML

You might be puzzled as to what this new factor consists of and why it is being included. Allow me to elaborate.

## AI Machine Learning As A Carbon Footprint

In a recent study done at the University of Massachusetts, researchers examined several AI Machine Learning or Deep Learning systems that are being used for Natural Language Processing (NLP) and tried to estimate how much of a carbon footprint was expended in developing those NLP systems.

You likely already know something about NLP if you've ever had a dialogue with Alexa or Siri. Those popular voice interactive systems are trained via a large-scale or deep Artificial Neural Network (ANN), a kind of computer-based model that simplistically mimics brain-like neurons and neural networks, and are a vital area of AI for having systems that can "learn" based on datasets provided to them.

Those of you versed in computers might be perplexed that the development of an AI Machine Learning system would somehow produce CFP since it is merely software running on computer hardware, and it is not a plane or a car.

Well, if you consider that there is electrical energy used to power the computer hardware, which is used to be able to run the software that then produces the ML model, you could then assert that the crafting of the AI Machine Learning system has caused some amount of CFP via however the electricity itself was generated to power the ML training operation.

According to the calculations done by the researchers, a somewhat minor or modest NLP ML model consumed an estimated 78,468 pounds of carbon dioxide emissions for its training, while a larger NLP ML consumed an estimated 626,155 pounds during training. As a basis for comparison, they report that an average car over its lifetime might consume 126,000 pounds of carbon dioxide emissions.

A key means of calculating the carbon dioxide produced was based on the EPA's formula of total electrical power consumed as multiplied by a factor of 0.954 to arrive at the average CFP in pounds per kilowatt-hour and as based on assumptions of power generation plants in the United States.

### Significance Of The CFP For Machine Learning

Why should you care about the CFP of the AI Machine Learning for an autonomous car?

Presumably, conventional cars don't have to include the CFP ML factor since a conventional car does not encompass such a capability, therefore the factor would have a value of zero in the case of a conventional car. Meanwhile, for a driverless car, the CFP ML would have some determinable value, and would need to be added into the total CFP calculation for driverless cars.

*Essentially, it burdens the carbon footprint of a driverless car and tends to heighten the CFP in comparison to a conventional car.*

For those of you that might react instantly to this aspect, I don't think though that this means that the sky is falling and that we should somehow put the brakes on developing autonomous cars, you ought to consider these salient topics:

- If the AI ML is being deployed across a fleet of driverless cars, perhaps in the hundreds, thousands, or eventually millions of autonomous cars, and if the AI ML is the same instance for each of those driverless cars, the amount of CFP for the AI ML production is divided across all of those driverless cars and therefore likely a relatively small fractional addition of CFP on a per driverless car basis.

- Autonomous cars are more than likely to be EVs, partially due to the handy aspect that an EV is adept at storing electrical power, of which the driverless car sensors and computer processors slurp up and need profusely. Thus, the platform for the autonomous car is already going to be significantly cutting down on CFP due to using an EV.

- Ongoing algorithmic improvements in being able to produce AI ML is bound to make it more efficient to create such models and therefore either decrease the amount of time required to produce the models (accordingly likely reducing the electrical power consumed) or can better use the electrical power in terms of faster processing by the hardware or software.

- For semi-autonomous cars, you can expect that we'll see AI ML being used there too, in addition to the fully autonomous cars, and therefore the reality will be that the CFP of the AI ML will apply to eventually all cars since conventional cars will gradually be usurped by semi-autonomous and fully autonomous cars.

- Some might argue that the CFP of the AI ML ought to be tossed into the CFP Made bucket, meaning that it is really just another CFP component within the effort to manufacture the autonomous car. And, if so, based on preliminary analyses, it would seem like the CFP AI ML is rather inconsequential in comparison to the rest of the CFP for making and shipping a car.

## Conclusion

There's an additional consideration for the CFP of AI ML. You could claim that there is a CFP AI ML for the originating of the Machine Learning model that will be driving the autonomous car, and then there is the ongoing updating and upgrading involved too. Therefore, the CFP AI ML is more than just a one-time CFP, it is also part of the ongoing grouping too.

Let's split it across the two groupings:

- Total CFP of a car = (CFP Made + CFP Disposal + CFP ML1) + (CFP FuelUse + CFP FuelGen + CFP ML2)

You can go even deeper and point out that some of the AI ML will be taking place in-the-cloud of the automaker or tech firm and then be pushed down into the driverless car (via Over-The-Air or OTA electronic communications), while some of the AI ML might be also occurring in the on-board systems of the autonomous car. In that case, there's the CFP to be calculated for the cloud-based AI ML and then a different calculation to determine the CFP of the on-board AI ML.

There are some that point out that you can burden a lot of things in our society if you are going to be considering the amount of electrical power that they use, and perhaps it is unfair to suddenly bring up the CFP of AI ML, doing so in isolation of the myriad of other ways in which CFP arises due to any kind of computer-based system.

In the case of autonomous cars, it is also pertinent to consider not just the "costs" side of things, which includes the carbon footprint factor, but also the benefits side of things.

Even if there is some attributable amount of CFP for driverless cars, it would be prudent to consider what kinds of benefits we'll derive as a society and weigh that against the CFP aspects. Without taking into account the hoped-for benefits, including the potential of human lives saved, the potential for mobility access to all and including the mobility marginalized, and other societal transformations, you get a much more robust picture.

In that sense, we need to figure out this equation:

- Societal ROI of autonomous cars = Societal benefits – Societal costs

We don't yet know how it's going to pan out, but most are hoping that the societal benefits will readily outweigh the societal costs, and therefore the ROI for self-driving driverless autonomous cars will be hefty and leave us all nearly breathless as such.

# CHAPTER 4

# PROTESTORS USE
# OF
# AI SELF-DRIVING CARS

# CHAPTER 4

## PROTESTORS USE OF
## AI SELF-DRIVING CARS

The news seems to be replete with stories of people undertaking protests these days.

Oftentimes, the protestors will organize beforehand and aim to disrupt an everyday kind of activity, while in other cases the protestors will target a specific event or occasion that they hope to disturb.

Their overarching aim is typically to get attention to their protest, along with potentially stopping or slowing down whatever it is they are interrupting.

You've undoubtedly seen the approach of protestors that mass flood themselves into a given space or location.

*Let's unpack that kind of protesting, and then I'd like to share with you a new way of performing those mass flooding techniques, which I predict (sadly) will gradually be appearing, namely via the use of self-driving driverless autonomous cars.*

### Ways To Protest And How They Work

How do protestors undertake the mass flood technique?

It can be done in a subtle and hidden manner, or via an overt and demonstrable means.

There's the hiding trick that involves appearing as though they are just part of the ordinary crowd and then subsequently announcing their protest.

This has been done at political rallies, blending into the assembled attendees and then suddenly shouting and making a commotion for their protest effort. Another frequently targeted venue is to go into a courtroom or a hearing room, sit quietly among others seated to attend, and at some point, make a clamor to disturb the proceedings.

Rather than the use of hiding, protestors can take a different tack and visibly amass, doing so with quite a noticeable flurry and commotion. They might then move around or proceed in a manner intended to get maximum attention and cause disruption. For example, protestors might communicate via social media to assemble say at the corner of 1st Street and 5th Avenue, and after a sufficiently sized crowd has appeared, they opt to march down 5th Avenue as a collective mass.

These various protest methods can range from being legal to becoming or being quite illegal.

In the United States, it is generally acceptable to carry out a protest, if a given jurisdiction's requirements have been legally satisfied. You might need to get a permit or take necessary steps to legally perform a protest.

Once a protest gets underway, it sometimes exceeds the legally allowed bounds and swerves into becoming an illegal effort, perhaps shifting into violent acts or other untoward actions. The protestors might not have sought to do so, but nonetheless they could have uncorked a bottle of improper protesting, inciting a mob-like mindset, and the next thing you know the activity has veered into a lawless act.

The protesting that I've been describing consists of protest actions in the real-world, which I mean to say exists in the physical everyday world that we inhabit. There is nowadays a rising use of the electronic world for protest purposes, commonly known as digital disobedience.

Note that I am not trying to suggest that the electronic world is the not in the real-world, since obviously the internet and social media are indeed real, and just trying to draw a bit of a distinction between protests that in a sense physically manifest themselves such as humans assembling on a street corner or in a courthouse and contrasting that to humans doing something similar online.

For those of you that are fans of the movie The Matrix, you might know what I mean when I suggest that there is a crossover from the "real-world" into the matrix-like electronic world (oops, spoiler alert!).

## Digital Disobedience And ECD Arising

Digital disobedience normally consists of performing online protest actions that aim to draw attention to the protest and simultaneously disrupt either some everyday online activity or an online special event.

When you ponder that definition, you'll notice that it is essentially the same as the physical protesting that I've been describing herein and merely shifted into the electronic online space.

A more formal title given to this digital disobedience is ECD, standing for Electronic Civil Disobedience, though some assert it really should be coined as Electronic Cyber Disobedience.

I'm betting that you've heard or known about situations whereby a website was "taken down" by having been overwhelmed with tons upon tons of rapidly fired electronic requests to the site. In computer security parlance, this is called a Denial of Service (DoS) kind of attack. Depending upon how it is carried out, the attack can also be described as a DDoS, a Distributed Denial of Service security hack.

Remember how I mentioned that human protestors could amass in the streets and perform a mass flood that would disrupt street traffic?

Well, the DoS and DDoS are the same kind of mass flooding, using electronic bits and bytes rather than people walking and running in the streets.

To amass people in the physical world would seem to be a rather simple and easy thing to do, simply notify prospective protestors and ask them to assemble at a particular place on a particular date and time. Pretty easy to implement if people are interested and willing to participate in the protest.

Well, it's relatively easy to do the same in terms of the electronic world, aiming to mass flood a website, and in some ways even easier than doing so in the physical world.

You can merely ask online for a ton of people to go ahead and try to access the website on the same specific date and time, all of them ready at their keyboard or smartphone to perform the protest, or more simplified would be for an individual or small set of such "protestors" to use computer automation as a means to carry out the attack (involving less online people, leveraging computers or bots to help do the mass flooding for you).

The electronic world and the physical world can be combined as a mass flooding or Denial of Service method via the use of self-driving cars.

### Self-Driving Cars As Unwitting Accomplices

Imagine that you want to undertake a protest at the corner of 10th Street and Pinole Avenue, seeking to form a crowd that will disrupt traffic and draw attention to your protest.

Once self-driving driverless cars are prevalent, it is assumed that we will be able to hail them for ridesharing purposes via our smartphones.

As such, you could ask fifty people to show-up at noon tomorrow at the designated street corner and have all of them at the precise noon hour all-at-once initiate requests for a self-driving ridesharing car to come pick them up.

This would presumably cause at least fifty self-driving cars to simultaneously attempt to converge on that specific street corner at nearly the same point in time. It would likely gum up traffic. Other traffic including human driven cars would get mired in the traffic snarl.

Those that sought to have the self-driving cars come to the spot might then try to keep the self-driving cars there, telling the AI that they need time to get into the now awaiting driverless car.

You might wonder whether you could pull that same trick today, doing so to human driven ridesharing cars. The odds are against it. If you had human drivers in ridesharing cars, they would likely get wise to what was taking place and it is doubtful that you would be able to either get the ruse to work or that it would last for very long.

You might argue that the ridesharing networking system ought to have detected that a mass of requests was happening all at once in the same location, and therefore should have gotten suspicious about the matter.

But, it's not so easy to ascertain that it isn't a legitimate act, since it could be that a concert or some local event has ended, and the attendees are all now seeking to get rides home.

Of course, a downside for the protestors is that they (in theory) would have to be registered on the ridesharing network and therefore their names and identifies would be known (this could be tricked). Also, they might need to incur a cost for having the self-driving cars come to pick them up, though this could also be dealt with via other sneaky electronic means.

Actually, in comparison to humans amassing in the streets, wherein the police could readily nab them or have video taken to later trace the protestors, the use of the self-driving cars as unwitting accomplices can potentially be done in a more surreptitious manner. The "protestors" could electronically conceal themselves if they were wise to how to do so.

There are numerous variants of this.

You might ask the AI to park the self-driving car in the middle of the street. This could then become a blockage for traffic and disrupt the other cars trying to use the road.

Interestingly, this brings up a key "ethics" or societal question that has yet to be addressed about driverless cars.

*Should humans be able to direct the actions of a self-driving car, telling the AI what to do, and if so to what degree is the AI supposed to obey such commands?*

If you are immediately thinking that it isn't right for a self-driving car to just park itself in the middle of the street simply because a human directed it to do so, I'd challenge you to consider whether the AI would know that it is a sensible thing to do or not do. There might be some very valid reasons that a human would park a car in the middle of a street, and the AI has no common-sense reasoning to decide whether the instruction is a proper one or not.

## Conclusion

The bottom-line is that self-driving cars could be dragged into use as a protest tool.

Though I had provided a scenario of fifty people on a street corner hailing driverless cars, it could be that those fifty people were actually spread around the globe and merely submitted their electronic requests as though they were standing on the street corner (tricking or spoofing their actual location).

Worse still, it wouldn't need fifty people and could be done potentially via one person alone, and again the person might not be anywhere physically near the street corner being used for the protest, perhaps sitting in their pajamas at home in their bedroom.

Some readers might be disturbed that I've brought up something that perhaps protestors would not have ever thought of, and thus somehow opened or revealed a pandora's box, allowing protestors to become cognizant of an idea about what they might do in the future.

I'd actually argue the opposite, and state quite fervently that I'm doing an important service by bringing up something that ultimately would have been stumbled upon, and that would otherwise have been an "unforeseen" nightmare which the automakers and tech firms would have had to figure out how on-the-fly they could cope with.

Sticking our heads into the sand about what self-driving cars portend for us is a risky and foolhardy proposition, I assert.

Instead, since true self-driving cars aren't here yet, it makes sense to bring up these aspects now, allowing for time to put in place cybersecurity methods to detect and prevent such actions.

I'd rather that we solve or resolve these kinds of hacktivism possibilities, beforehand, rather than all of us getting caught "unawares" because we didn't think carefully about how self-driving driverless cars will change the world as we know it today.

Let's take the red pill, now, and not fall for the blue pill (oops, another spoiler alert reference to The Matrix).

# CHAPTER 5

# ROGUE BEHAVIOR
# AND
# AI SELF-DRIVING CARS

# CHAPTER 5

## ROGUE BEHAVIOR

## AND

## AI SELF-DRIVING CARS

A recent news item decried a seemingly bizarre but true story involving a woman that was run over by her own vehicle.

While driving her car, she was threatening to shoot some trespassers on her property and one of the intruders opened her car door to apparently grab the gun, she fell out and was run over because the car was still in gear and went in motion (her foot was no longer on the brake pedal). She survived with leg injuries and was briefly hospitalized.

Would you say that the vehicle deliberately rolled over her leg?

I don't think that many would ascribe a foul intention to the vehicle.

You could say that it was her fault as a driver that she exited the vehicle without putting it into park, though she was apparently caught off-guard and didn't have time to carefully disengage the gears.

No matter how the untoward encounter occurred, there is a bit of irony whenever someone's own car perchance runs them over, doing so in the case where there is no one driving the car at the time of the incident. These situations happen from time-to-time and catch our attention, perhaps because we often tend to think that our cars might have a mind of their own.

People anthropomorphize their cars, ascribing human-like qualities to their prized vehicles. We give pet names to our cars. We gingerly bathe our cars via taking them to pricey car washes. We sometimes adore our cars when they get us quickly to our desired destinations. We can as readily loathe our cars when they breakdown on hectic freeways in the middle of scowling traffic.

Here's an intriguing question: *Could a self-driving car go rogue?*

True self-driving cars are going to be imbued with an AI system that is acting as the driver of the vehicle. The story about the woman that got run over entailed a car that had no driver at the time and was simply mechanically in gear and mindlessly proceeding forward. If cars are going to have AI systems at the wheel, maybe they could run over someone and do so for either intentional or unintentional reasons.

Let's unpack the matter.

## Levels Of Self-Driving Cars

It is important to clarify what I mean when referring to true self-driving cars.

True self-driving cars are ones that the AI drives the car entirely on its own and there isn't any human assistance during the driving task.

These driverless cars are considered a Level 4 and Level 5, while a car that requires a human driver to co-share the driving effort is usually considered at a Level 2 or Level 3.

The cars that co-share the driving task are described as being semi-autonomous, and typically contain a variety of automated add-ons that are referred to as ADAS (Advanced Driver-Assistance Systems).

There is not yet a true self-driving car at Level 5, which we don't yet even know if this will be possible to achieve, and nor how long it will take to get there.

Meanwhile, the Level 4 efforts are gradually trying to get some traction by undergoing very narrow and selective public roadway trials, though there is controversy over whether this testing should be allowed per se (we are all life-or-death guinea pigs in an experiment taking place on our highways and byways, some point out).

Semi-autonomous cars require a human driver, and yet such cars could indeed run over the very human driver that is responsible for the driving of the car.

How could that happen?

One obvious example involves semi-autonomous cars that are outfitted with a remote driver summons capability, which Tesla has recently opted to rollout (see my piece here about the dangers of the Tesla summons feature).

The driver can stand outside of the car, such as standing at the curb near a restaurant door, and remotely turn-on their car that's parked in a nearby parking lot. Using a special app on their smartphone, the human can then "drive" the car to their standing position, directing the car to drive to them via buttons and switches visually portrayed on their cell phone.

In theory, the human using the smartphone is still considered the driver of the car, even though the car might be guided by ADAS automation that instructs the vehicle to back out of the parking spot and drive throughout the parking area to try and reach the human summoning it.

If the car manages to get confused, it could indeed run into the human that's summoning it.

There are plentiful videos online that show Tesla's that are at times nearly hitting pedestrians or other cars during the summon activity, or that have actually hit someone or something (luckily, for now, doing so at low speeds and tending to not incur any substantive injuries or property damage).

In the case of true self-driving cars at the Level 4 and Level 5, the possibility of having the car hit someone or something is quite real, especially since there is no human driver involved in guiding or preventing the car from doing so.

When I make such a statement, those in the self-driving car industry get instantly riled-up because they point out that human drivers hit people and things all the time. Yes, that's absolutely true. Sadly, there are about 40,000 deaths caused by car crashes each year in the United States, and an estimated 2.5 million injuries via car-related incidents.

All I'm saying is that the belief that self-driving cars will do away with all car crashes and incidents is rather farfetched and unrealistic.

My tag line has been that zero fatalities is a zero chance of happening.

Presumably, true self-driving cars will radically reduce the number of car deaths and injuries, and aiming to reach zero is a laudable goal, but let's not mislead the public into believing that the number will drop to zero. It won't.

Of course, every life saved, or injury avoided that might have been incurred due to a human driver is a blessing and we can rejoice if self-driving cars are able to achieve those savings.

## Determining Rogue Behavior

What does it mean to say that someone has exhibited rogue behavior when driving a car?

Suppose I told you that a driver the other day opted to maneuver their car up onto the sidewalk.

This certainly seems like an obvious example of rogue driving.

We aren't supposed to drive cars on sidewalks.

Pedestrians on sidewalks could get hit. Artifacts such as fire hydrants and postal boxes could get smashed into by a car on the sidewalk. All in all, driving onto sidewalks only seems to occur in movies wherein they are trying to dramatize a character that is going outside the bounds of normal driving behavior.

Imagine though that the car drove onto the sidewalk due to the road being closed, as a result of a car accident, and furthermore that a cop was directing cars to slowly go onto the sidewalk and drive around the accident scene. Pedestrians were prevented from being on that portion of the sidewalk and the cars were slowly and carefully using the sidewalk as a temporary path.

Is that rogue driving?

Probably not.

Some pundits define rogue driving as any type of illegal driving act, but this doesn't seem to be an especially robust way to define rogue aspects. You could argue that driving on the sidewalk was an illegal act, though it was perhaps made legal or at least allowable due to being instructed by an authority figure (the duly authorized police officer).

There is also the matter of whether a rogue act while driving causes any actual harm or not.

Some suggest that if a rogue driving maneuver doesn't lead to anyone getting hurt, and there's no property damaged, it isn't a rogue situation. This definition doesn't seem especially satisfying since it would appear to allow rogue driving actions that could happen anywhere and at any time if the act perchance did not lead to any adverse outcomes.

One other factor involves the intent of the driver.

It becomes a rather murky matter if you say that rogue driving must be intertwined with some form of foul intent. A driver that opts to drive down an alleyway at 50 miles per hour and endangers people and things, well, were they intending to cause that endangerment or were they innocently driving down the alley, perhaps unaware of the dangers they were creating.

For ease of discussion herein, let's go with the notion that rogue driving consists of any driving action that violates societal norms and expectations for the proper driving of a car, excising intent from the definition, and the rogue effort can range from being highly egregious to minimally egregious in terms of adverse outcomes (the magnitude only referring to the severity of the rogue action and not whether the act is considered a rogue effort).

For true self-driving cars, the intent aspect comes up quite a bit due to the voiced concern that someday we might have sentient AI, and potentially the AI would have "intent" akin to humans. When we reach that vaunted point, some decry that the AI could arise and decide to start running over humans, perhaps doing so out of spite or maybe to rid the world of humans.

I can assure you that we are eons away from having sentient AI and therefore I am not going to entertain the aspects about AI with that kind of human-like intent (for some interesting AI conspiracy theories, see my posting here).

## Self-Driving Car Rogue Acts

Consider the myriad of ways that a true self-driving car could commit a rogue driving act.

Keep in mind that the rogue driving act as defined herein is without intent per se and deals with violating societal norms of driving.

- A self-driving car could veer out of its lane and threaten another nearby car, one that's being driven by a human driver.
- A self-driving car could take a tight turn at a corner and nearly hit a pedestrian standing there.
- A self-driving car could ram into a car ahead that has come to a sudden stop due to debris in the roadway.
- Etc.

It might be shocking to think that those kinds of driving actions by a true self-driving car could ever occur, particularly since the media oftentimes portrays that self-driving cars will be perfect drivers. By a magical incantation, self-driving cars will seemingly never do anything that could imperil other cars or pedestrians.

It's troublesome that the media makes such outlandish assertions. Please be aware that those portrayals are utterly out-of-whack and regrettably are establishing false expectations that no viable self-driving car and no automaker could achieve.

How could such rogue driving actions be performed by the AI of a truly driverless car?

Here's a sampling of the ways that these actions could happen:

- **Bugs Or Errors.** The software that's on-board the self-driving car could contain a bug or error, one that escaped being caught during testing. Sadly, the bug could arise at the worst of times and lead to the AI making a bad choice in the midst of a life-or-death real-time driving act.

- **Bad Programming.** AI software can contain programming logic that is not a bug and nor an error per se, and instead was thought to provide the right kind of effort when executed, yet nonetheless, when an edge or unusual circumstance arises, the software takes action that we all would agree is not a desirable choice.

- **Machine Learning Runs Afoul.** Much of the AI for self-driving cars consists of Machine Learning or Deep Learning software that has been trained based on patterns found in lots of driving-related data. Often, the automaker or tech firm has no direct means of ascertaining why the AI has opted to take various actions (an acknowledged issue involving the lack of XAI, known as explainable AI). Unfortunately, Machine Learning might have found a pattern that only makes sense in a specific context, yet the AI doesn't embody the contextual elements needed.

- **Hardware Glitches.** The AI on-board the driverless car is being executed on computer processors akin to the computing that you find in your smartphone or laptop, though often juiced up and much faster than everyday personal computers. There is always a chance that the computer processors or the electronic memory could suffer a glitch, for which in the middle of a driving act could have untoward consequences.

- **Sensors Issues.** The sensors on a driverless car act as the eyes and ears of the AI system. If the sensors are obscured by dirt and mud, they might not convey a proper indication of the surrounding scene. The sensors can wear out, they can misreport data, and otherwise suffer from any number of system-related difficulties. The AI might become blind to the roadway or worse still get false readings about what is or might not be ahead of the vehicle.

- **System Overwhelmed.** A self-driving car could potentially get overwhelmed during the driving act. Imagine if the driverless car is zooming along at 80 miles per hour, doing so amidst lots of other cars, and the driving scene is a hairy mess. A car ahead gets hit by a rock that fell off a truck and bounces onto the roadway. All the cars get into a frenzy. Was the AI system stress-tested for these kinds of all-out mania driving situations?

- **Implanted Virus.** One of the greatest worries expressed about self-driving cars is the chance that a computer virus could get planted into driverless cars. A handy aspect of driverless cars is that they will be using OTA (Over-The-Air) electronic communications to get the latest updates pushed to them, but this also provides a conduit for a mass virus to be sneakily shoved into self-driving cars.

- **Hack Attack.** In addition to the implanting of a computer virus, another cyber-security concern is that a human hacker might be able to crack into a driverless car. Self-driving cars are going to be using V2V (vehicle-to-vehicle) electronic communications, which is helpful so that one driverless car could warn another one that a cow is standing in the middle of the highway up ahead. On the other hand, a hacker in a car next to you might be able to send commands to your self-driving car via V2V that could commandeer your vehicle and allow the hacker to do dastardly things.

- **Human Remote Operators.** Some automakers are going to allow a remote human operator to intervene in the driving task of a driverless car. I've warned that this is opening a can of worms and that teleoperations of a true self-driving car should not be a safety case. Nonetheless, for those automakers that do opt to allow a remote human operator to take over the driving, this could be troubling due to the remote operator getting disconnected during a crucial moment, or other miscues might undesirably occur.

## Prevention And Mitigation

Society is unlikely to accept true self-driving cars if the chances of rogue acts happening raises the ire of us all, including that regulators would likely be spurred to action to suppress or stop driverless car rollouts.

A key obligation for self-driving carmakers is to try and stridently prevent and mitigate the odds of rogue activities by their driverless cars.

Per the Uber deadly incident in Phoenix last year, all it takes is one bad apple, so to speak, and the rest of the barrel can get spoiled.

Many would agree that the Uber incident generated a backlash that has partially slowed or at least made for more cautious efforts by many of the automakers and tech firms in the driverless car industry. Some say it didn't do enough and we are still at unfettered heightened risks.

Ways to try and deal with the emergence of rogue acts in driverless cars include:
- Tightened cyber-security for all external connections
- Cyber-protecting the cloud-based OTA
- Revisiting systems security across the automotive ecosystem
- Implementing fail-safe features for on-board hardware
- Self-detecting sensors that realize when they are awry
- Real-time double-checking of AI driving commands
- Extensive simulation to test beyond roadway efforts
- Wide-ranging closed track or proving ground testing
- Boosting of spending and attention to driverless car QA
- Putting in place a high-level Corporate Safety Officer
- Instill in the AI developers a safety-first mindset
- Etc.

## Conclusion

In the intense pressure to get a self-driving car onto our roadways, the automakers and tech firms could be spurred into cutting corners.

Everyone wants to get the acclaim and attention from being the first to "win" at the driverless car moonshot-like race.

Furthermore, the cost to undertake the numerous preventatives or mitigating approaches for undercutting rouge actions is expensive and time-consuming. When push comes to shove, and since driverless cars are still a draining R&D effort, there is a temptation to cut back now and assume that later you'll add-in the "bells and whistles" to ensure greater safety.

Nobody can end-up affording that kind of thinking.

The societal reaction will clamp down on progress toward driverless cars. Firms that opt to prematurely release their self-driving cars will ultimately get sued, likely putting them out-of-business once those lawsuits succeed.

As Homer famously warned in *The Odyssey*, one rogue is usher to another still. For true self-driving cars to succeed, we must pull out all the stops and seek to prevent or mitigate rogue driving actions.

.

# CHAPTER 6

# USING HUMAN DRIVERS VERSUS

# AI SELF-DRIVING CARS

# CHAPTER 6

# USING HUMAN DRIVERS VERSUS
# AI SELF-DRIVING CARS

If you build it, they will come.

Maybe yes, maybe no.

In the ever-evolving field-of-dreams effort to create true self-driving cars, a key assumption by nearly everyone is that people will flock to using driverless cars.

It seems perhaps blatantly obvious that anyone with half a brain will choose to use an AI-driven self-driving car in lieu of getting cranky, emotionally laden, fallible and maybe smelly human driver to take them for a ride.

Imagine, if you will, there you are, standing on a downtown street corner, aiming to use your mobile app to request a ridesharing lift.

You've had a long day at work and want to sit quietly in a car that will drive you home. Upon pulling up the app, there is a choice offered to select either a ride that is a driverless car versus being able to choose a car driven by Avery Smith (a driver that is unknown to you, other than they have a high Yelp-like rating as a driver).

Which would you choose?

Assume for the moment that all else is equal about the driving aspects, except for the fact that one car is being driven by an AI system while the other choice is a car being driven by a human. Pretend that the cost is the same, the driving performance is the same, the level of driving safety is the same, and so on.

I realize those are rather gigantic assumptions, which I'll break somewhat later herein, but go with me for now about the thought-provoking scenario involved.

If you are exhausted after a day of interacting with people at work, you might be tempted to use the driverless car. There won't be a human driver at the wheel that will try to find out how your day was or ask what your hobbies might be, or perhaps try to annoyingly entertain you with banter about the weather.

In a self-driving car, it's just you and the AI.

Similar to an Alexa or Siri, you can pretty much tell the AI where you want to go, and if the AI starts to pepper you with cute stories or other Natural Language Processing (NLP) interaction, you can firmly instruct it to shut-up.

Sure, you can tell a human driver to likewise shut their mouth, though in the back of your mind there is a hint of concern that doing so could upset the driver.

Might an upset driver become a riled-up driver?

Could a riled-up driver be more likely to make a mistake while driving you home?

Could the human driver go completely nuts and drive you and the car into a ditch, doing so merely because, well, because the driver lost their mind and opted to call it quits on this earth?

Yes, those are the potential adverse outcomes whenever you get into a car and have someone else (another person) driving the car.

You are at the mercy of the human driver.

Some people claim that if they noticed a human driver veering out of control, it would be a simple matter to reach over to the steering wheel and abruptly take over the car.

Really?

This might happen in movies, but I dare say that anyone attempting to take control of a car from a human driver is going to have a difficult time doing so and most likely will incur a deadly result. Plus, if you are seated in the backseat of the car, you'd need to be a human contortionist and have the speed of The Flash to get into the front seat and magically grab the driving controls before all heck broke loose.

This all certainly seems to suggest that you'd be prudent to select the driverless car over the human-driven car.

It's also partially why there is such a strong belief and assumption that once true self-driving cars become available; people will flock to using them.

Here's then the shocking news for you: *There's a chance that people might not flock to driverless cars.*

Why does that matter?

The automakers and tech firms are spending billions upon billions of dollars to try and accomplish the moonshot-like goal of achieving true self-driving cars. Right now, those efforts are funded almost entirely via R&D dollars that are flowing out the door, non-stop, bleeding profusely, one might say, and there isn't any noticeable incoming revenue to match the tremendous costs being incurred.

Suppose the vaunted self-driving car is indeed built and fielded yet suppose further that the ridership is spotty.

I'm not saying there won't be any ridership and instead suggesting that the ridership might be less than entirely fulfilling. Rather than the base assumption that every minute of every self-driving car is going to involve toting around passengers, imagine that riders were opting to sometimes use a driverless car and sometimes use instead a human-driven ridesharing car.

Yikes, those automakers and tech firms could lose their shirts!

After all their tireless efforts, and upon pouring vast amounts of monies into the presumed pot-of-gold investment, if the income is only a trickle and people are not obsessed with using a driverless car, the result could be financially devastating, possibly inducing bankruptcy for some that heroically persevered and pioneered us into a world of self-driving cars.

But, you protest, isn't it apparent that people will undeniably flock to self-driving cars?

Can't we put aside any qualms of that one-in-a-zillion chance that a few of the unwashed might cling to using human-driven cars over adopting the use of AI-driven cars?

There's always some Luddites that won't leverage new tech, and as such, it is tempting to accede to the notion that a tiny segment of society won't use driverless cars, becoming like those that insisted on using a horse and buggy when automobiles first came on the scene.

Let's unpack the matter.

## The Levels Of Self-Driving Cars

It is important to clarify what I mean when referring to true self-driving cars.

True self-driving cars are ones that the AI drives the car entirely on its own and there isn't any human assistance during the driving task.

These driverless cars are considered a Level 4 and Level 5, while a car that requires a human driver to co-share the driving effort is usually considered at a Level 2 or Level 3. The cars that co-share the driving task are described as being semi-autonomous, and typically contain a variety of automated add-ons that are referred to as ADAS (Advanced Driver-Assistance Systems).

There is not yet a true self-driving car at Level 5, which we don't yet even know if this will be possible to achieve, and nor how long it will take to get there.

Meanwhile, the Level 4 efforts are gradually trying to get some traction by undergoing very narrow and selective public roadway trials, though there is controversy over whether this testing should be allowed per se (we are all life-or-death guinea pigs in an experiment taking place on our highways and byways, some point out).

Since the semi-autonomous cars require a human driver, such cars aren't particularly significant to the question of ridership in true self-driving cars. There is essentially no difference between using a Level 2 or Level 3 versus a conventional car when it comes to providing a ridesharing service.

It is notable to point out that in spite of those idiots that keep posting videos of themselves falling asleep at the wheel of a Level 2 or Level 3 car, do not be misled into believing that you can take away your attention from the driving task while driving a semi-autonomous car.

You are the responsible party for the driving actions of the car, regardless of how much automation might be tossed into a Level 2 or Level 3.

## Choosing The Type Of Driver

For Level 4 and Level 5 self-driving cars, you are going to have a disembodied AI system that will be your chauffeur.

In theory, the AI system won't get drunk and won't get weary while driving a car. This is considered a cornerstone of the rationale for pursuing true self-driving cars.

No more drunk drivers, at least via AI-driven self-driving cars.

No more human fallible drivers that snap and opt to drive into a roadside barrier.

Human judgment and human prerogatives will go out the window and driverless cars won't get angry, they won't be thinking about the ballgame they are missing due to driving people around to make some dough, and they won't turn their heads to talk with you in the backseat (potentially a human driver might do so, failing to then notice a double-parked truck that they are about to slam into).

Let's splash some reality though into the Utopian beliefs about the advent of self-driving cars.

First, true self-driving cars are not going to miraculously appear overnight and suddenly replace all conventional cars.

There are 250 million conventional cars in the United States alone, and they aren't going anywhere soon. The economic cost to discard all those conventional cars is astronomical. The cost and effort to produce and field self-driving cars are going to be huge, meaning that driverless cars will incrementally and progressively emerge, though at a likely gradual pace.

All in all, you should expect that there will be a mixture of human-driven cars and self-driving cars and that gradually and slowly an increasing number of self-driving cars will appear on our roadways, yet for a lengthy and enduring period of time they will both exist on our streets (there's also an open question about whether human driving will ever be completely eliminated).

The significance of this undeniable mixture will be that driverless cars are still going to get into car accidents, often involving a human-driven car that rear-ends a self-driving car or a driverless car that rams into a human-driven car that swerved directly into the path of the AI-driven vehicle.

Therefore, you are not somehow attaining absolute driving safety by selecting a true self-driving car.

The risks of a driverless car getting into an accident will not be zero, of which there are some pundits that keep saying we are headed to a zero fatalities world due to the advent of driverless cars. I've said repeatedly it is a zero chance of attaining zero fatalities.

Even if we were to wave a magic wand and do away with all human-driven cars, you'd still have those pesky human pedestrians that can decide to dart in front of a moving car. A driverless car cannot overcome the law of physics. If a human opts to leap into the street and there was no means to earlier enough detect the impulsive action, a human fatality is likely to be produced.

This then takes us to a quite crucial factor in your choice of a human-driven car versus a driverless car.

Safety.

Is it safer to take a driverless car that might regrettably get intertwined with a human-driven car, and be caught unawares during the driving act, or might a human driver have done a better job at anticipating the actions of other human drivers and avoided the car accident altogether?

When I earlier said that you were to assume that the safety capabilities of a self-driving car and a human-driven car were equal, this is a yet ascertained element or factor.

We already know and accept the idea that human drivers differ in their safeness of driving a car. Not only does one human sometimes drive more safely than another one, your safeness can vary every time that you get behind a wheel.

If you are well-rested and feeling good, perhaps you are a fully attentive driver. Stayed up late last night and you just got word that you were fired at work, well, you might be a rather bad driver for the remainder of that day.

Despite our collective realization that human drivers vary significantly in their safeness, we shrug this off and get onto the roadways.

In the case of self-driving cars, I'll put aside the numerous ways in which they can falter or fail, including that there might be hidden bugs or errors, there might be a computer virus implanted, etc.

Those are all possibilities and therefore you'll ultimately need to weigh those aspects into your decision about choosing to ride in a self-driving car.

I'm trying to momentarily simplify the matter to provide a focus on what seems like the most paramount of considerations.

## Making A Choice Over And Over

Returning to the general notion of safeness, I hope you can see that driverless cars won't be enwrapped in a supernatural cloak of safety.

As you stand there on a downtown street corner and try to decide which car to request for your ride home, you will be torn between using the driverless car, which has some advantages over human-driven cars, versus using the human-driven car (which has some advantages over driverless cars).

To clarify, each has various advantages and disadvantages in comparison to each other.

In short, there isn't a slam dunk and outright obvious answer to which you would or should choose.

That's why the automakers and tech firms are currently sitting on a bit of a razor's edge.

If they build it, meaning the building of true self-driving cars, will people indeed use those driverless cars?

I'm already acknowledged herein that people will undoubtedly use driverless cars, but the unknown is how many people will do so, and how frequently they will do so.

You've stepped out of a bar and it is past midnight. Not wanting to deal with a human driver, you select a driverless car. You aren't especially thinking about which is safer in any driving sense, and instead, you are considering that the driverless car omits the hassle of a human driver that might rankle you about being drunk.

Somewhat cloudy minded due to partially being inebriated, you nonetheless logically choose the self-driving car.

Consider a different situation.

You are going to send your kids to school and cannot drive them there, so you decide to use a ridesharing service.

Having a human driver would mean there is a chance that the adult driver might (let's hope not!) mess with your kids, so you decide to take a chance instead of the driverless car. You realize that the kids being alone in a self-driving car has its own downsides, but at least you've taken the adult driver out of the equation.

These are various realistic situations wherein people might select a self-driving car over using a human-driven car.

Let's look at the other side of the coin.

You are in a hurry and need to get to your destination as rapidly as possible.

Those quaint driverless cars that you've used before are programmed to be legally abiding, acting squeaky clean while driving on public streets and byways. A human driver is bound to cut corners and drive you at a hurried pace, especially if you offer them a hefty tip.

So, you opt to go with the human driver.

Makes sense.

Consider another example.

You haven't been feeling well and you fell and hurt your leg recently.

It is difficult for you to get around. If you choose a self-driving car, you'll need to get into it on your own. You've found in the past that when a human-driven car pulls up to your house, the human driver realizes that you are limping and oftentimes gets out of the car to help you into the car.

Best to go ahead and choose the human driver as your selection for the ridesharing service.

These kinds of use cases are aplenty.

We don't know how much of the time that people will choose the driverless car versus the human-driven car.

Automakers and tech firms could be surprised to find that people aren't flocking to the use of driverless cars.

Whoever owns the driverless cars might also be shocked.

Suppose that a company buys a fleet of driverless cars and puts them into use. This company doesn't have any human-driven cars in its fleet and has decided that driverless cars are the way to go.

Another company is using human drivers for its fleet.

I ask you; which company stands to make more money?

If you yell out voraciously that it will be the company with the driverless cars, I'd say you might want to reread the commentary herein. No such guarantee exists.

Should firms have a mixture of driverless cars and human-driven cars in their fleets?

Maybe, though it all depends upon a myriad of factors.

Let's consider some of those factors.

### Wrapping Up On The Choice

Will the price that you pay as a passenger when using a driverless car be the same as the price that you would pay for the use of a human-driven car?

Nobody knows.

I earlier pretended that as a base assumption the costs were the same for both a self-driving car and a human-driven car, so let's now undo that assumption.

You are standing on the street corner, looking at your mobile app, and the price for the driverless car is (let's say) more than the human-driven car, so which do you choose?

Alternatively, you look at your mobile app and the price of the human-driven car is higher than the driverless car, so which do you choose?

Another factor could be the timing and availability elements.

The nearest driverless car is ten minutes away from you, while a human-driven car is two minutes away from you.

Which do you choose?

On and on we can go.

There are many characteristics and considerations that will go into your mental calculus about whether to choose the use of a self-driving car versus a human-driven car.

Toss out the false imagery of driverless cars all cruising around in abundance and serving as your only choice.

Instead, passengers are going to weigh their options between using a driverless car versus a human-driven car and make their choices, moment to moment, depending upon what seems best at the time of their making such a choice.

Automakers and tech firms that assume an assured "build it and they will come" are setting themselves up for a bit of a disappointment, along with quite arduous challenges after we cross that bridge.

If we can get to the end of the rainbow and actually produce true self-driving cars, will they turn out to be profitable?

For now, please keep seeing those rings of gold and remain hopeful that driverless cars will mint money.

# CHAPTER 7

# TESLA HODGE-PODGE ON AI SELF-DRIVING CARS

# CHAPTER 7

# TESLA HODGE-PODGE
# OF AI SELF-DRIVING CARS

Elon Musk is gutsy and often swings for the fence in terms of stretching the bounds of engineering and science.

That's a big plus.

Unfortunately, his marketing zeal and perhaps innate optimism seems to do battle with his learned physics acumen and ability to employ any semblance of Mr. Spock like logic (see my piece about how his physics training might be paradoxically undermining his self-driving car efforts).

Yesterday, during the Tesla earnings call, he managed to enlighten and simultaneously confound on exactly what the status of their efforts are toward achieving a true self-driving car.

It was a mishmash covered in hodge-podge.

Get ready for the roller coaster ride about his comments, which veered from heartily suggesting an imminent release of true self-driving to then, well, not really, and a series of what could be (politely) considered walk-backs.

As you'll in sense in a moment, part of the problem in understanding his remarks is that the words he is choosing to use are pretty much made-up and lack any definitive meaning for the rest of the self-driving tech world.

Maybe the words mean something to him, and he can certainly call an apple a poiq'lid if he so desires, but without conforming to the standards accepted by just about everyone else, whatever he says becomes conveniently malleable, likely to mislead, and unable to be appropriately relied upon.

Tesla fans: *Don't get upset with me, instead try to get Musk to use regular English and tell us what he means in something other than seemingly proprietary versions of Vulcan or Ferengi.*

**What Was Said**

Let's start with one of his remarks about the so-called full self-driving mode in a "feature-complete release" (which might be an apple or an orange, no one can say for sure):

"While it's going to be tight, it still does appear that will be at least in limited early access release of a feature complete self-driving feature this year."

Yikes!

We can try to parse that sentence, but we'll need to use a decoder ring to do so.

There are essentially two key elements, one being whatever the capability being delivered consists of, and the other involves the timing of the delivery of that capability.

The timing part seems the easiest to decipher, so let's tackle it first.

The phrase "limited early access release" would seem to imply that a beta version is coming, and for which only a select few Tesla owners are going to be able to participate in the beta.

The phrase "this year" certainly seems straightforward, presumably, the beta would appear between now and December 31, 2019, giving Tesla these next two months to get the beta out-the-door.

Case closed on the timing aspects; it would seem.

Not so fast.

Adding some additional clues about the timing, Elon Musk further commented that the timing is "not for sure" but that he believes that it "appears to be on track" to go into the limited release by the end of this year.

If you want to be generous, you could say that his indication that he wasn't sure about the timing is merely reflective of how hard a problem it is to craft a true self-driving capability. These things take time. Maybe he can be allowed some wiggle room, you might argue.

On the other hand, the convenience of adding the "not sure" nugget is that he can later say that he never definitively said it would happen by the end of this year. For those that don't like politic speech, the toss-it-in of the "not sure" would seem to be a warning sign. It's a hedge that perhaps reveals the reality that it is unlikely by the end of this year.

Anyone that has followed Musk's promises on the timing of getting things done would already know that any dates offered need to be taken with a grain of salt (a rather huge grain).

In any case, as already mentioned, you can interpret the loosie goosey remarks in whatever world view you wish to adopt.

We haven't though yet gotten to the real loosie goosey stuff.

The next tortuous parse involves surfacing the capability that the timing was presumably referring to.

Apparently, they will be released in beta a capability that will consist of a "feature complete self-driving feature."

Nobody (other than Musk, perhaps) knows exactly what that means.

Is it a true self-driving car, or something less so?

Round up the topmost fifty experts in self-driving cars, lock them in a room, and ask them to tell you what "feature complete" of a "self-driving feature" might be.

Besides the blank stares due to the opaqueness of the language used, you'll get a cacophony of interpretations that range across the entire landscape of what a self-driving car might consist of.

To try and make sense of the mumbo jumbo, let's first clarify what the rest of the world uses to express the capabilities of self-driving cars.

Once we have that on the table, we can then try to figure out where the "feature complete" of a "self-driving feature" might fit into the preferred and globally accepted language.

### The Levels Of Self-Driving Cars

True self-driving cars are ones that the AI drives the car entirely on its own and there isn't any human assistance during the driving task.

These driverless cars are considered a Level 4 and Level 5, while a car that requires a human driver to co-share the driving effort is usually considered at a Level 2 or Level 3. The cars that co-share the driving task are described as being semi-autonomous, and typically contain a variety of automated add-ons that are referred to as ADAS (Advanced Driver-Assistance Systems).

There is not yet a true self-driving car at Level 5, which we don't yet even know if this will be possible to achieve, and nor how long it will take to get there.

Meanwhile, the Level 4 efforts are gradually trying to get some traction by undergoing very narrow and selective public roadway trials, though there is controversy over whether this testing should be allowed per se (we are all life-or-death guinea pigs in an experiment taking place on our highways and byways, some point out).

Most everyone agrees that the existing Tesla's are Level 2's.

It is notable to point out that in spite of those dolts that keep posting videos of themselves falling asleep at the wheel of a Level 2 or Level 3 car, do not be misled into believing that you can take away your attention from the driving task while driving a semi-autonomous car.

You are the responsible party for the driving actions of the car, regardless of how much automation might be tossed into a Level 2 or Level 3.

## The Cryptic Words

When Tesla refers to its moniker of "Full Self-Driving" or FSD, you undoubtedly think this must be a reference to a Level 4 or Level 5 true self-driving car.

Maybe, maybe not.

Furthermore, adding to the murkiness, Musk has been augmenting the scope of FSD to include the verbiage of it being "feature complete."

So, we have a made-up moniker of "Full Self-Driving" that has on top of it the made-up qualifier of being "feature complete."

Does a feature complete FSD mean that it is more complete than some version of FSD that does not feature complete?

Everyday deductive logic seems to suggest so.

Taking a look at the official web site of Tesla, here's what it says about FSD:

"Autopilot enables your car to steer, accelerate and brake automatically within its lane. Full Self-Driving Capability introduces additional features and improves existing functionality to make your car more capable over time."

Try to match this rather ambiguous Tesla and Elon Musk terminology to the everyone-else accepted definition of Level 4 and Level 5.

This so-called "Full Self-Driving" is apparently something that makes your car more capable over time, but capable to what degree?

To the degree that is defined by Level 4?

To the degree that is defined by Level 5?

The vagueness of FSD as a meaningful term renders it unable to be matched to the standards and therefore becomes less meaningful (some would say meaningless) moniker.

Worse still, it uses common words such as "full" and "self" and "driving" that imply things that aren't apparently the case at all. This makes it a dangerous moniker, offering a populace-assumed meaning that doesn't comport with what it genuinely involves.

Going further, it could be that FSD refers to Level 3 and doesn't even reach the vaunted true self-driving of Level 4 and Level 5 at all.

In short, we have Elon Musk's comments consisting of a promised delivery of a beta by the end of this year, though the "not sure" put that into limbo, which will consist of a capability that is ill-defined and can be whatever they decide to deliver.

What is especially scary is that some of the media picked up on Musk's comments and ran headlines that said full self-driving for Tesla's could arrive by the end of this year.

Say what?

I suppose you can legitimately claim that those were the words Musk used, but it could mean that Tesla is delivering Level 3 by the end of this year, or maybe it is Level 4, or maybe it is Level 5.

It is important to not fall into the wording trap of merely repeating the unclear made-up words, which have a populace-assumed meaning when those words are so variously interpretable.

I would be willing to bet that 99% of lay people that read such a headline would immediately assume that it means that Tesla is delivering Level 5 by the end of this year.

Not going to happen.

There is absolutely no evidence whatsoever to support the possibility of Tesla releasing Level 5 by the end of this year.

There is equally little to essentially no evidence that they can get to Level 4 by the end of this year.

Not meaning to be the bearer of bad news, but it seems quite questionable that they could get to a true Level 3 by the end of this year, though it is possible that they could achieve some salient aspects of Level 3.

During the question and answer period of the call, Musk added some semblance of clarity to his earlier remarks, though still leaving lots of room for interpretation.

Generally, it seemed that he defines feature complete FSD to be a capability of being "autonomous but requiring supervision and intervention at times."

Well, if that's really what the gobbledygook phrase means, you can readily rule out that the capability is going to be a Level 4 or Level 5.

The use of the word "but" after the word "autonomous" is a watchword that should clue us that he's referring to a semi-autonomous capability, and not a true and unqualified fully autonomous capability.

During his answer to another question, he then said that the feature complete FSD won't be "reliable enough that you do not need to pay attention, in our opinion" until sometime at "the end of next year."

You could drive a Mack truck through that word web that leaves a gaping hole about when a true self-driving car capability will arise.

## Conclusion

Despite the breathless headlines that have said there is a Tesla "full self-driving car" capability potentially being released this year in beta, I'd suggest we all take a heedful breath and consider what really seems to have been stated.

Hold on while I bring back the decoder ring.

By Musk's own admission, the upcoming release, which might or might not happen this year, will apparently be semi-autonomous and not truly autonomous (recall his qualifying the word "autonomous" with the crucial "but" part, and granting that human intervention will be required in the driving task, thus no better than a Level 3 capability).

Thus, there might be some semblance of a Level 3 coming up.

Getting to a Level 4 or Level 5 is apparently being aimed by the end of 2020, though the aspect that Musk said it would be "reliable enough that you do not need to pay attention, in our opinion" provides once again a tremendous amount of wiggle room.

Specifically, the "in our opinion" could be interpreted that Tesla and Musk hope it will be autonomous, though maybe it might not turn out to be, even though they were hoping it would be.

Or, if you want to be generous, perhaps the "in our opinion" means that they believe that others might not agree that the autonomous capability is truly autonomous, such as by governmental officials that might test the capability and ascertain that it really doesn't meet the proper definition of autonomous.

The "in our opinion" too is kind of a backhanded slap at such government officials, implying that those darned nitpicky government officials could put the kibosh on something that Tesla and Musk believe to be autonomous, and yet is "falsely" undermined by bureaucrats that don't know what they are doing.

It's an easy dig against "the man" and one that would appeal to many that relish Musk's pirate-like willingness to break the conventional rules in the tech trope of always wanting to move fast and break things (appealing to those that embrace disruption and transformation).

You should ask yourself this: *Can the beloved mantra of move fast and break things be sensibly applied to self-driving cars?*

Keep in mind that self-driving cars are going to be on our public roadways.

They can kill and injure those inside the self-driving car, and kill and injure those in other nearby cars, and kill and injure nearby pedestrians, and bicyclists, and the like.

The especially unfortunate aspect of talking in these exasperating riddles about self-driving cars by prominent car tech celebrities is that it can confuse the myriad of stakeholders involved, including the general public, it can confound regulators, it can cause an unwarranted backlash against other automakers and tech firms in this space (why aren't we as far along as Musk, yet this reaction is based on a mirage rather than what is actually proven to be the case), and so on.

Tesla and Musk have a vital role in advancing the state of self-driving cars.

This is more than simply a tech-oriented role.

They also need to recognize and realize that the world looks upon them to provide insights and guidance about the true pace of true self-driving car advancements.

Avid followers of Star Trek know that the Ferengi will do and say just about anything to attain a profit.

Vulcans live by logic and reason, attempting to minimize emotion.

We need to have all self-driving car leaders be willing to gain sahrafel (the Vulcan word for trust) with the full range of self-driving car stakeholders, both inside and outside the industry, along with being brave enough to speak yeht'es (the Vulcan word for truth) about how far along their self-driving cars efforts really are.

Live long and prosper, it's an important and life bolstering phrase to live by.

# CHAPTER 8

## SOLO OCCUPANCY

## AND

## AI SELF-DRIVING CARS

# CHAPTER 8

# SOLO OCCUPANCY

# AND

# AI SELF-DRIVING CARS

Today's ridesharing via Uber and Lyft is presumably supposed to get more people to share rides and therefore cut down on the number of trips made, along with making more efficient use of cars and roadways, plus saving the earth by knocking down the volume of harmful exhaust emissions.

Unfortunately, contemporary ridesharing is more akin to ride-hailing than it is to actual ride sharing.

By-and-large, people using present-day ridesharing services are taking trips that encompass just one passenger, themselves. They are hailing a ride that will transport themselves, only, and not sharing the ride with any other passengers (a scant one-fifth of the time they opt for sharing a ride).

Of course, there is another person in the car, the driver, but that person is not a passenger per se and resides in the car for the purpose of driving the vehicle.

Various industry stats suggest that the number of occupants in ridesharing cars is around 1.5, which includes the driver.

This is a disheartening number and raises uncomfortable questions about the promises of ridesharing.

Worse too is the aspect that a significant percentage of the travelers have reported via surveys that they would have walked or ridden a bike (around 10% of riders say so), but they were wooed instead to use a ridesharing option due to the ease of doing so.

And, worse upon worse, nearly one-third to almost one-half reported that they would have taken a form of mass transit if the ridesharing approach wasn't so readily available and relatively inexpensive.

Ride-hailing has usurped the spark to walk or bike and undercuts the forces toward using mass transit.

Originally, it was believed that ridesharing might be the so-called "last mile" means to connect people from their homes to mass transit. The idea was that you would have a ridesharing car take you to a bus stop or train station, and you'd continue the remainder of your journey via mass transit.

That's not a notable element in today's leveraging of ridesharing services.

People are doing transit substitution, opting toward using ridesharing cars in lieu of other modes of transit.

Who can blame them?

We all relish the single occupancy aspects of driving our own cars, and the next best thing is being the sole passenger in a ridesharing car.

As a result of catering to our desire to travel in our own bubble, the ride-hailing tsunami has not reduced the number of trips that people make, it has not gotten more people to take trips together, and it isn't saving the earth by polluting less.

Arguments are often made that ride-hailing has done the reverse of those good things.

People are making more trips via cars than they did before (as mentioned, avoiding walking, biking, and mass transit). Short trips that once were done via another mode are now done via a car.

There is also the sneaky aspect of induced demand too.

With induced demand, people can be induced into traveling more than they would have otherwise traveled before.

Suppose you usually went to the grocery store on a once per week basis. You only went once a week because getting there was a hassle.

Now, via the easy of using your smartphone, you can seamlessly request a ridesharing car and travel to the grocery store numerous times per week. Thus, your one trip per week blossoms to say three or four trips per week.

The congestion produced by all these added trips is rather noticeable on our roads, particularly in popular places that are constrained such as a crowded downtown area or an airport pick-up lane.

From an infrastructure perspective, some analysts indicate that the heightened volume of essentially single-occupancy (just one passenger) of ride-hailing is going to savage our streets and highways, tearing them up by the increased traffic flow, doing so at a faster pace than ever before.

All in all, this kind of false ridesharing (merely ride-hailing) is a downer, and something should be done about it.

Voila, one might exclaim, pundits tell us that a solution is indeed on the horizon.

Here's the solution and a probing question about it: *Will true self-driving cars finally bring about ridesharing and overcome the tendency of riders to do only ride-hailing?*

Let's unpack the matter.

## The Levels Of Self-Driving Cars

It is important to clarify what I mean when referring to true self-driving cars.

True self-driving cars are ones that the AI drives the car entirely on its own and there isn't any human assistance during the driving task.

These driverless cars are considered a Level 4 and Level 5, while a car that requires a human driver to co-share the driving effort is usually considered at a Level 2 or Level 3. The cars that co-share the driving task are described as being semi-autonomous, and typically contain a variety of automated add-ons that are referred to as ADAS (Advanced Driver-Assistance Systems).

There is not yet a true self-driving car at Level 5, which we don't yet even know if this will be possible to achieve, and nor how long it will take to get there.

Meanwhile, the Level 4 efforts are gradually trying to get some traction by undergoing very narrow and selective public roadway trials, though there is controversy over whether this testing should be allowed per se (we are all life-or-death guinea pigs in an experiment taking place on our highways and byways, some point out).

Since the semi-autonomous cars require a human driver, such cars aren't particularly going to alter the dynamics of the per capita occupancy aspects. There is essentially no difference between using a Level 2 or Level 3 versus a conventional car when it comes to the number of people that might be riding in the vehicle.

One assumes that the industry metric of the Average Vehicle Occupancy (AVO) will remain the same as it is today (unless other factors come to play that are outside of the fact that the car happens to be a Level 2 or Level 3).

It is notable to point out that in spite of those dolts that keep posting videos of themselves falling asleep at the wheel of a Level 2 or Level 3 car, do not be misled into believing that you can take away your attention from the driving task while driving a semi-autonomous car.

You are the responsible party for the driving actions of the car, regardless of how much automation might be tossed into a Level 2 or Level 3.

## What Happens With Autonomous Cars

A true self-driving car will not have a human driver since it is instead being driven by the AI system.

Yay!

We will henceforth be able to keep track of the number of passengers as its own measure and not need to include any accounting for a human driver.

You might be wondering why the pundits believe that driverless cars will boost the number of passengers per trip.

One aspect often cited involves the interior space availability of a true self-driving car.

Currently, the tryouts of driverless cars tend to involve a conventional car that has been augmented with self-driving tech capabilities. There is still a steering wheel, even though the AI doesn't need it, and likewise there are pedals for braking and acceleration that aren't needed either (the AI handles the driving controls under-the-hood, one might say).

Future designs of driverless cars are envisioned to rip out the driver's seat and all the driving controls, freeing up the interior of soon to be high-tech cars.

You could put swivel seats into the opened-up space, allowing passengers to face each other or swivel in whatever direction they cared to look.

In theory, the redesigned seating and openness will encourage more people to ride together.

I'll be the skeptic in the room and offer that just because you build it, you can't also assume that people will use it in the manner that you dream of. All that openness could potentially go to waste.

Furthermore, some designs are incorporating seats that layout into beds, allowing you to catch a nap while heading to work. The seat-into-bed aspect could make a single occupant that much happier to have the space to stretch out and catch some needed shuteye. If so, you certainly don't want a noisy or annoying fellow passenger that's going to undermine your catnap.

Some believe that you'll be working in your driverless car, doing so throughout the day. You'll do so with work colleagues, all of you sitting in the swivel seats, perhaps arrayed around a small worktable, and be heading to various company offices, warehouses, and other locales.

One question to ask about these changes in passenger habits is whether this is going to take the place of existing trips or will it be more akin to induced demand that expands the number of trips?

Nobody knows.

Another rosy prediction via optimistic pundits is that people will get to know other people that they didn't already know, doing so via the commuter-like aspects of sharing a driverless car ride.

Yes, you might do more of the Uber or Lyft style pooling once there are true self-driving cars, or you might not.

Ironically, the openness of the interior space of the car might cause people to be more reluctant to share the space.

Right now, in conventional cars, we all need to squeeze into our bucket seats and are kept tightly in place. It's not easy to be overbearing or obnoxious, though some try.

With the added roominess inside driverless cars, will people become more insufferable in their seating and deployment of annoying habits?

On airplanes, we tend to be squeezed into seats, yet there is still the opportunity to get up and go to the bathroom or stretch your legs. This can be disruptive to fellow passengers that are seated near you. The same kind of surly attitudes and foul behavior that you see on planes or (even worse) subways trains might infect self-driving cars.

Imagine heated arguments over the use of a worktable or the uncaring outstretch of one's legs that happens to bump up against another passenger. Rude behavior can arise in driverless cars just as it can anywhere else that people are forced into tight proximity of each other.

Not wanting to be overly pessimistic about human behavior, but it is also possible that people might physically confront or attack each other while inside a self-driving car.

Your first thought is that people don't do so in conventional cars, so why would they suddenly change into beasts while inside a driverless car?

Keep in mind that there isn't a human driver in a driverless car.

Those human drivers in everyday cars tend to be a highly visible yet silent signal that you should remain constrained and polite while inside the car. We are conditioned as a society that the driver is the captain of the ship and their dictum shapes our in-car behaviors.

Plus, in the back of our minds, we know that any disturbance in a human-driven car could distract the driver. If we distract the driver, they might run into a pole or crash into another car. Once again, the driver serves as an ever-present dampener of uncivilized activities inside the vehicle.

I'm not saying that all of today's passengers are swayed by this logic, but it seems reasonable that most riders are.

In a driverless car, there is not a human driver to dampen the outrageous outbursts or bouts that might ensue.

Are we doomed to anarchy inside a self-driving car?

Probably the largest factor to curtail outlandish behavior will be the candid camera that's likely to be included in a self-driving car.

Most self-driving cars will be outfitted with a camera that points inward, allowing for capturing on video of a rider that tries to trash the interior of the car. That same camera will be like Big Brother watching you, perhaps providing some semblance of behavioral guardrails, though unlike a human driver that can turn around and bop you, there's not much the AI can do to stop the fisticuffs that might be taking place.

At least the AI can tattle on those that are getting into fits, and perhaps even route the driverless car to the nearest police station or rendezvous with a police car that's nearby.

## Conclusion

An especially significant factor concerning the conundrum of ridesharing versus ride-hailing for self-driving cars will be the cost of riding in the driverless car.

Today's human-driven ridesharing services are relatively inexpensive, partially due to the ridesharing services eating a chunk of the cost and wanting to build market share over profit right now.

Nobody is sure what the cost per ride or per mile will be to use a true self-driving car.

If the cost is relatively high, it would presumably shift people toward sharing rather than riding alone. Passengers might be willing to put up with the lack of privacy and the doldrums of being around other people, doing so to share the cost of using a driverless car.

There is an interesting calculus involved in this matter.

It is important to realize that self-driving cars will not suddenly overtake the existing population of cars. In the United States alone there are 250 million conventional cars, and those cars aren't going to disappear overnight.

In short, there will be a mixture of human-driven cars and driverless cars, which will gradually and inexorably likely shift over time toward more and more driverless cars.

Meanwhile, you'll be able to make a reasoned choice, namely do you use the self-driving car or a human-driven car for your ridesharing trips?

At first, people might be enamored of self-driving cars and seek to use a driverless car whenever they utilize ridesharing. My guess is that the initial excitement and novelty will wear-off. At that point, the cost will loom as the crucial factor (in essence, at first, the cost might be acceptably high, since people are getting the thrill of being inside a driverless car, part of the bargain for the heightened price).

Passengers will eventually be considering the day-to-day trade-off aspects of using an AI-driven car versus a human-driven car and assuming all else being equal, the cost might be the final arbiter.

Indeed, some pundits decry that self-driving cars will be only used by elites that can afford to do so (see my piece that debunks that one-sided argument and presents alternative views on the matter).

If we wave a magic wand and get people to behave and ride in driverless cars with their fellow humans, it might be possible to arrive at a vaunted modernized AVO of say 2, meaning that the average number of passengers has reached two (no drivers, two actual passengers).

This would be astounding since it would mean that in the aggregate, we would have to also counterbalance the rides of solo passengers by a like number of rides with three or more passengers.

Can we do it?

I'd like to hope so, but it's probably not worth holding your breath over, since people will be people, and unless we undergo a dramatic cultural shift, it sure seems people to like to ride along on their own.

Just them and their friendly AI driver.

# CHAPTER 9
# EINSTEIN'S TWINS PARADOX AND
# AI SELF-DRIVING CARS

# CHAPTER 9

# EINSTEIN'S TWINS PARADOX
# AND AI SELF-DRIVING CARS

Ask any physicist about the infamous twin paradox problem and you are likely to find yourself facing a lengthy diatribe about the topic.

Often referred to as Einstein's twin paradox, Einstein was known for focusing on the nature of time and clocks, doing so as part of his theories on relativity, so the topic can be referred to as the Einstein clock paradox rather than mentioning twins per se (historians point out that the origins of the thought experiment can be traced to scientist Paul Langevin in a 1911 paper that he wrote and in which he used twins for the earlier framing of the problem).

What exactly is the paradox, you might be wondering?

Imagine that you are standing here on earth, which I assume most of you are, and you happen to have been born with an identical twin. Your beloved twin has decided to become an astronaut and venture into the far reaches of outer space.

You are both the age of 25, let's say.

You wave goodbye as your twin rockets away. Pretend that the spaceship is incredibly fast, so fast that it moves at nearly the speed of light.

Marking the days on your calendar here on earth, your twin flies for 25 years to a far point in the universe, turns around, and for another 25 years flies back to earth.

Upon arriving here on earth, you greet your long traveling twin, embracing with a firm hug.

I'll ask you a seemingly simple and innocent question: *What is your age and what is the age of your twin upon meeting each other at the end of your twin's voyage?*

Well, we know that you marked the days and believe that the trip took 50 years. The trip started when you both were 25 years old. Therefore, the rote math suggests that you are now 75 years old and that presumably your twin is also 75 years old.

Suppose I told you that your twin is now actually only 30 years old, having aged a mere 5 years while you have aged fifty years.

Is that shocking to you or does it comport with what you would have expected?

If you've ever watched any science fiction movies about space travel, you've undoubtedly seen story after story that involves a space traveler experiencing time more slowly than those of us on earth. When they get back to earth, their children are older than they are, and the peers that they left on earth are now long deceased.

I'm guessing that you, therefore, accept the premise that your twin would be younger than you and have aged more slowly than you.

Not everyone would necessarily agree with that premise.

Your basis for believing that your twin aged more slowly is that they traveled at a fast speed and therefore approached our fundamental unit of time per the speed of light.

The paradox aspect is that we could turn the situation around and say that instead of looking at the twin that flew away from you, suppose we look at things in the eyes of your twin and they would perceive that you essentially flew away from them. You might say that the twin was "stationary" and you here on earth were moving away from the twin.

In that case, maybe you ought to have aged only five years and your twin should have aged fifty years.

That is the crux of the paradox.

Which is it, did you age the fifty years or did your twin age the fifty years?

Of course, you might toss your hands in the air and say that you are both still the same age, regardless of how many years passed, since you could try to argue that both of you aged the same number of years while the traveling occurred (those that undertake such hand tossing are considered "deniers").

Most of today's physicists would agree that the "correct" answer is that you aged fifty years and your twin aged the five years.

For such physicists, there isn't any paradox and the answer easily is derived via Einstein's theory of special relativity and using too the handy Lorentz factor (a vital equation for figuring out elapsed time based on your velocity and number of years traveled).

Here's what Einstein said: "If we placed a living organism in a box … one could arrange that the organism, after any arbitrary lengthy flight, could be returned to its original spot in a scarcely altered condition, while corresponding organisms which had remained in their original positions had already long since given way to new generations."

Note that you don't need to use twins in this thought experiment and could substitute the twins by simply saying that you have two clocks that are set to the same time, of which you then send one of the clocks on the journey, and upon returning the traveling clock to earth you compare the time of the two clocks.

In fact, the entire twin's story can be reduced to the belief that moving clocks go slower (a matter of time dilation, as it were).

Mentioning twins makes the tale a bit more entertaining. It is partially used to suggest that the two items being compared are to be as nearly identical as possible, aiming to reduce any side arguments about the fact that maybe something different in the two originating elements can account for a time difference.

You are welcome to mull over the paradox and study it with whatever intensity and gusto you prefer.

For purposes herein, the infamous problem brings up the overall notion that time can be perceived differently and on a relative basis for an observer or participant seem to be longer or shorter in length.

Here's an intriguing question: *Could the advent of true self-driving cars cause us to have a different sense of time?*

Don't misinterpret the question to somehow suggest that self-driving cars are going to move at the speed of light. Sorry, that's not in the cards for now.

Self-driving cars might though subtly alter our sense of time via the convenience and ease of transit via car travel, changing our perception about time.

Let's unpack the matter.

**The Levels Of Self-Driving Cars**

It is important to clarify what I mean when referring to true self-driving cars.

True self-driving cars are ones that the AI drives the car entirely on its own and there isn't any human assistance during the driving task.

These driverless cars are considered a Level 4 and Level 5, while a car that requires a human driver to co-share the driving effort is usually considered at a Level 2 or Level 3. The cars that co-share the driving task are described as being semi-autonomous, and typically contain a variety of automated add-ons that are referred to as ADAS (Advanced Driver-Assistance Systems).

There is not yet a true self-driving car at Level 5, which we don't yet even know if this will be possible to achieve, and nor how long it will take to get there.

Meanwhile, the Level 4 efforts are gradually trying to get some traction by undergoing very narrow and selective public roadway trials, though there is controversy over whether this testing should be allowed per se (we are all life-or-death guinea pigs in an experiment taking place on our highways and byways, some point out).

Since the semi-autonomous cars require a human driver, such cars aren't particularly going to alter the dynamics of time perception. There is essentially no difference between using a Level 2 or Level 3 versus a conventional car when it comes to the time paradox aspects.

It is notable to point out that in spite of those dolts that keep posting videos of themselves falling asleep at the wheel of a Level 2 or Level 3 car, do not be misled into believing that you can take away your attention from the driving task while driving a semi-autonomous car.

You are the responsible party for the driving actions of the car, regardless of how much automation might be tossed into a Level 2 or Level 3.

## True Self-Driving Cars And Time Perception

For the use of Level 4 and Level 5 driverless cars, there isn't a human driver in the car. Occupants inside the self-driving car are all considered passengers.

When you get into a self-driving car, the AI system will whisk you away to whatever destination you've stated. No need on your part to watch the road. No need to provide driving advice about which way to go. You can liken this to acting as a passenger in an airplane, whereby you simply sit back, relax, and the traveling occurs without you having to lift a finger.

Suppose you want to visit a good friend that lives twenty miles away from you.

Normally, you'd need to grab up your prescription glasses, make sure you have your valid driver's license on you, and then drive your car to see your friend. During the driving journey, you'd be stressed out about the horrid traffic and the near misses with ornery drivers.

By the time you reached your friend's place, you'd be exhausted, irritable, and exasperated at the drive. As such, you might vow to your friend that it will be a rare day that you opt to drive to see them again, given the arduous nature of getting there. The trip seemed to take forever.

Switch to a scenario involving the use of a driverless car.

You get into the self-driving car and have no worries about whether you can see the road, and nor do you have a driver's license on you or even need one at all. During the trip, you watch some streaming videos and enjoy the time spent in the self-driving car. In fact, you might recline the seat and take a nap, dreaming perhaps about time travel and someday visiting planets at the far reaches of our galaxy.

In the former case of driving the car, time seemed to go slowly, agonizingly so.

In the latter case of being a passenger in a self-driving car, time seemed to move along quickly.

Even your friend might perceive the time differences of your taking a self-driving car versus having driven yourself.

Upon your arrival at your friend's place when you drove a car, you are vocal in complaining about the drive, and your friend feels terrible that you had to endure the long drive.

When arriving via a self-driving car, you are refreshed and happy, so your friend feels like it was just moments ago that you said you'd be on your way.

In short, your perception of time could change as a result of making use of self-driving cars. Likewise, your friend, not having traveled in the driverless car, might also perceive time differently as a result of your using a driverless car.

Again, this is not to suggest that time changed in some manner as a result of the self-driving car.

Instead, the emphasis is on the perception of time by both the participant and the observer.

## Conclusion

If this change in a sense of time can occur, one argument to be made is that presumably via today's ridesharing services you would already be undergoing that same change in time perception.

A ridesharing service of today allows you to sit back and relax since there is a human driver at the wheel.

The comparison is only half-right.

You still need to be wary about the human that is your ridesharing driver. In theory, the human driver could make wayward moves and crash the car. Being in a ridesharing car is not the same as being absent of all concerns about the driving task.

For self-driving cars, some assert that they will be entirely safe and never crash. I don't subscribe to that belief. There will still be car crashes, though (hopefully) of a much smaller volume and a lesser force of damage or injury, though we don't yet know if that will be the case.

Assume for the moment that driverless cars eventually will be extremely safe and safer than human drivers in the aggregate. In that case, the claim is that you'll be less on-edge when in a driverless car and more prone to being able to enjoy the ride without any substantive qualms.

Another factor is that self-driving cars will gradually be rolled-out and there will be a mixture of both conventional cars and driverless cars on our roadways for many years to come.

One could contend that you'll sometimes be using a human-driven car and other times be using a self-driving car.

The use of conventional cars will continue to remind you of the "time" related aspects and therefore continue to keep the driverless car perception as a fresh one. Eventually, the number of conventional cars will presumably dwindle, and you'll only rarely use a human-driven car.

In that case, you'll inevitably get used to being inside a driverless car.

Over time, we will all become used to the self-driving car as this time-saver or time enabler. A new normal will inexorably take hold of us.

At that juncture, we will no longer perceive the time of travel as any different since it will all be of the same nature. Our time perception will have adjusted.

That's admittedly a long time from now, so let's enjoy our new perception of time as it unfolds, relishing it for as long as time will allow.

# CHAPTER 10

# NATION-STATE TAKEOVER

# OF

# AI SELF-DRIVING CARS

# CHAPTER 10

# NATION-STATE TAKEOVER

# OF

# AI SELF-DRIVING CARS

The 50th anniversary of the Internet was recently celebrated by those that trace the origins of the vaunted worldwide web to the first time that a message was transmitted on the ARPANET (a forerunner to the Internet), occurring on October 29, 1969 at UCLA and in connection with the Stanford Research Institute (known today as SRI).

Philosophically, most of those involved in the development of the Internet was hoping that having a global means to electronically communicate might lend itself to greater freedom on this earth.

When people get to know each other, presumably the chances of treating each other as inanimate objects and discounting their humanity is lessened.

There was some heartfelt cheering going on when the Internet was later used as a means for accelerating revolutions that overcame dreadful oppression. Famous instances of pro-democracy grassroots efforts using the Internet that ultimately toppled untoward governments are exactly the kind of people-power catalyzing capabilities that were envisioned

Technology typically though is a dual-edged sword.

You can be freed by the sword, and yet you can also be imprisoned by the sword.

Currently, there is a concern that digital nationalism is beginning to take hold.

Countries can opt to craft an immense electronic Great Firewall that prevents those within that specific country to readily connect with people outside of that country. Special "kill switches" can be established too, allowing the government of a country to quickly disconnect any efforts to go electronically beyond the borders of the country by citizens that are stretching out their necks.

Besides restricting access, a government might also dictate what kind of content will be allowed onto the country-constrained Internet. Undesirable content can be electronically detected and removed. Electronic filters can attempt to inhibit access. Freedom of expression becomes only the kind and amount of expression that the government declares suitable.

On top of those disquieting aspects, the government can also use the Internet to trace the activities of its citizens. Personal privacy becomes lacking when the government keeps track of what online sites you've visited and with whom you are online communicating.

Those of us that use the Internet each day in everyday ways are ingrained in the assumption of a fully open and globally far-reaching Internet and are shocked and taken aback at the very idea that a country might turn the tables on the Internet and make it into a foreboding tool of government control and public repression.

I'd like to briefly switch topics and then tie together seemingly disparate topics that are perhaps surprisingly quite related.

Efforts are underway by tech firms and automakers to create the next generation of cars. We are on the verge of having true self-driving cars, ones that are driven by AI and there is no human driver involved.

There are a lot of hoped-for pluses that are expected to come along with true self-driving cars.

Presumably, driverless cars will be in a lot less car accidents, reducing immensely the 40,000 deaths and 1.2 million injuries that occur in the United States alone each year. Furthermore, mobility will be expanded via self-driving cars to include those that are today mobility disadvantaged. All in all, it seems like driverless cars will be a societal godsend.

Time to tie together two key topics.

Here's the question to seriously ponder: *Could a nation-state decide to take over the self-driving cars that are within its sovereignty?*

Just as digital nationalism involves taking over the Internet by a country, a likewise act could possibly occur involving a country that takes over all the vaunted driverless cars within its borders.

Yes, it can occur.

Yikes!

Let's unpack the matter.

### The Levels Of Self-Driving Cars

It is important to clarify what I mean when referring to true self-driving cars.

True self-driving cars are ones that the AI drives the car entirely on its own and there isn't any human assistance during the driving task.

These driverless cars are considered a Level 4 and Level 5, while a car that requires a human driver to co-share the driving effort is usually considered at a Level 2 or Level 3. The cars that co-share the driving task are described as being semi-autonomous, and typically contain a variety of automated add-ons that are referred to as ADAS (Advanced Driver-Assistance Systems).

There is not yet a true self-driving car at Level 5, which we don't yet even know if this will be possible to achieve, and nor how long it will take to get there.

Meanwhile, the Level 4 efforts are gradually trying to get some traction by undergoing very narrow and selective public roadway trials, though there is controversy over whether this testing should be allowed per se (we are all life-or-death guinea pigs in an experiment taking place on our highways and byways, some point out).

Since the semi-autonomous cars require a human driver, such cars aren't particularly going to alter the determination of where cars go, since human drivers will remain in the driver's seat (of course, a government could nonetheless regulate the driver's as to monitoring them and dictating where they can drive, but this is a gargantuan kind of control that is hard to implement and enforce).

There is essentially no difference between using a Level 2 or Level 3 versus a conventional car when it comes to the nationalism topic.

It is notable to point out that in spite of those dolts that keep posting videos of themselves falling asleep at the wheel of a Level 2 or Level 3 car, do not be misled into believing that you can take away your attention from the driving task while driving a semi-autonomous car.

You are the responsible party for the driving actions of the car, regardless of how much automation might be tossed into a Level 2 or Level 3.

## True Self-Driving Cars And Control

For the use of Level 4 and Level 5 driverless cars, there isn't a human driver in the car. Occupants inside the self-driving car are all considered passengers.

The AI system that's on-board the driverless car is doing the driving.

Updates to the AI software are undertaken via the use of OTA (Over-The-Air) updating, consisting of the car initiating an electronic connection with a cloud-based service and downloading the latest system patches.

The OTA is also used to upload data that has been collected by the self-driving car.

Data that can be uploaded include the sensor collected data that is being captured by the cameras of the self-driving car, along with data coming from the radar, LIDAR, thermal imaging, ultrasound, and any other sensors mounted to the vehicle as an aid in the AI performing the driving task.

In addition, there are likely to be cameras pointing inward into the interior of the driverless car.

If you own a self-driving car and are allowing it to be used in a ridesharing service, you'll want to know whether any passengers happen to mark graffiti or tear-up those expensive leather seats. And, if your children are riding in a driverless car to school, you'd feel better about them riding in the no-adults-present self-driving car by being able to watch the kids on your smartphone during their driving journey.

Not all self-driving cars will be the same.

This comes as a surprise to many people that seem to think that the tech firms and automakers are all taking the same approach to devising true self-driving cars.

Instead, each brand or model of a self-driving car will likely have its own proprietary way of performing the driving task.

That being said, the odds are that most driverless cars will be operating in somewhat the same ways. They all need to abide by the driving laws and driving rules to sufficiently be roadway capable on our public streets.

Pundits are predicting that self-driving cars will be primarily owned in fleets. A large company such as an automaker or a ridesharing firm or any other entity will buy a flock of driverless cars and put them around town for use on a ridesharing basis.

Despite the aspect that the self-driving cars might be somewhat distinct by model or brand, and despite the aspect that flocks might be owned by various companies, there is one thing that all driverless cars will likely have in-common.

The in-common element is that the driving will be performed by an on-board AI system, and furthermore that the on-board AI system can be changed via OTA, along with the data collected by the driverless car being pumped-up to an online cloud someplace.

So what, you might ask?

Here's the rub, and it's a big one.

*A nation-state could decide that any of the self-driving cars within its sovereignty must abide entirely by the wishes of the government.*

If any automaker or tech firm didn't want to comply, the nation-state could kick those cars out of the country.

The government might take such steps in a slow and gradually ratcheting up manner or might wait until driverless cars are relatively well-established in its domain and then try a midnight takeover if you will.

What makes the whole takeover aspect feasible is the point that the driver is a piece of automation and the automation can be established and changed remotely.

A kind of perfect storm for a government that wants to control its people.

## The Chilling Impacts

In theory, the government could decide whether Jane or Joe can use a self-driving car, perhaps denying them any kind of car-related usage or might dictate where Jane or Joe can be driven to by the driverless cars.

To keep the public from avoiding the strong arm of the government, a nation-state might ban all human driving, forcing everyone that wants to use a car to use a government-controlled driverless car.

The government can grab the voluminous data being gathered by the sensors of the driverless cars and aggregate it to get a large-scale indication of where its people go.

Keep in mind that the sensors are like a roving video camera, and when you have millions of cars crisscrossing your city or town, you could stitch together a rather comprehensive understanding of not just where the cars go, but also whatever the cars see wherever they go (such as you standing at a street corner or playing ball in your front yard with your children).

Furthermore, the government might insist that the inward-facing cameras be continually videotaping whatever happens inside the driverless cars. This video could be uploaded via the OTA and the government might use it in nefarious ways.

Imagine that people riding in these government zombie cars would need to be extremely cautious in what they say while sitting inside the self-driving car. There every utterance could be readily examined and used against them by the government.

This is a form of digital nationalism that goes beyond the online world and reaches directly into the physical and everyday world.

If this doesn't already send chills up your back, I'll add another equally scary thought.

You are riding in a self-driving car and have told the AI that you are heading to the grocery store. The AI replies that yes, it will drive you to the grocery store.

Along the way, you are looking at your smartphone and reading some emails and playing a fun online game.

The AI seemingly reaches your destination and suddenly two-armed government officials open the door of the driverless car.

Turns out that the government has decided that you are a wanted person.

You were easy to find because the moment that you got into the driverless car the facial recognition knew who you were. The AI communicated with the cloud, and the government then notified some goons to meet you at your destination.

Of course, the AI could have been directed to simply take you straight to a government detention center, rather than taking you to the destination that you thought you were going to.

Scary upon scary, it would seem.

## Conclusion

It is easy to write-off this kind of self-driving car nationalism or governmental take over as utterly fanciful and could never happen.

Maybe even place the idea into one of those crackpot conspiracy theory buckets about AI.

I'd say that you ought to rethink that assumption.

First, let's be clear that I'm not saying the AI becomes sentient and opts to take over. Instead, the AI is merely a form of automation that is dependent upon humans that run the overall aspects.

The humans in-charge of the AI software for the self-driving cars and that are responsible for the OTA are, well, they are humans, and subject to the whims of their government.

In that manner, this takeover theory is about a socio-political matter, more so than a technical-only matter.

The technology makes the Pandoras box possible, and it is the human element that can open the box.

Second, it is important to emphasize that this would most likely occur within a nation-state.

This would not necessarily be widespread among many nations and instead be limited to those governments that have an oppressive will and are able to control the freedom of their people.

As such, you might end-up with most nations having driverless cars that roam freely and are not being government-controlled. Meanwhile, a smaller set of nation-states that can do so are bound to see the opportunities in nationalizing their driverless cars.

Third, you might be tempted to claim that no rightful thinking automaker or tech firm would ever allow this to occur.

That's a debatable contention.

Sure, presumably many or most of the automakers or tech firms might insist that such a takeover won't be allowed. If their driverless cars are already in the nation-state that wants to do the takeover, the automaker or tech firm might "brick" the self-driving cars and null out the onboard AI and turn-off the OTA.

On the other hand, if there are firms that were working closely with the government all along, those firms might either find themselves in a slippery slope fashion allowing a takeover to occur or might be woven into the government such that there really is no independence about how the driverless cars are to be utilized.

Fourth, you might believe that humans could fight back.

Of course, if the people within the nation-state decide to revolt against the government takeover, the people would likely be able to reinstitute "freedom" among the self-driving cars in that nation.

Would hackers be able to usurp the government control of driverless cars?

There's an irony involved in asking such a question.

Right now, most are worried that hackers will be able to break into self-driving cars and get the AI to do their bidding. To prevent this, automakers and tech firms are supposed to be building all sorts of cyber protections and security mechanisms to prevent such intrusions.

The irony, of course, is that we are herein asking whether "good attackers" that want to turn the "imprisoned" driverless cars into "freedom" driverless cars could hack their way into doing so.

The answer should be no, since if the hackers cannot get into the rightful self-driving cars, the same barriers should be preventing the hackers from getting into the nefarious self-driving cars.

Some might say this is all a tempest in a teapot.

All you need to do is provide an override for humans to take over a driverless car. In that manner, if a human doesn't like the government controlling the self-driving car, the human merely hits a button and voila, the human is now driving the car.

Sorry, that's a rabbit hole.

I won't go into all of the details, but the moment you allow humans to drive a driverless car, it no longer is a true self-driving car, and you are back to square one about the notion of autonomous cars.

Okay, you say, but at least allow the human to command the AI rather than the government. Oops, that's not going to work either because the human in the vehicle might be untoward or have untoward intentions.

On and on it goes.

You might (believe it not) offer that maybe the AI ought to be sentient, in which case it would just say no to the government oppressors. That's a bit of funny commentary since there are many AI conspiracists that insist that once AI becomes sentient it will imprison or kill us all.

Anyway, let's not all panic just yet.

I hope though that this discussion about the potential of a nation-state takeover is enough to spark intelligent debate about how the self-driving tech that is perceived by most to be neutral is, as always, something that can be turned toward the good of mankind or toward the bad of mankind.

Nation-states that are eager to find additional means to control their people are ready to pounce on the advent of driverless cars.

Nation-states that are excited about the opportunity to extend mobility and reduce car crashes are ready to adopt and accept driverless cars.

It's up to the people to help shape which way the self-driving cars go, including whether driverless cars are a freedom boon or a form of freedom bondage.

You decide.

# CHAPTER 11

# QUANTUM COMPUTERS

# AND

# AI SELF-DRIVING CARS

# CHAPTER 11

# QUANTUM COMPUTERS

# AND

# AI SELF-DRIVING CARS

Quantum supremacy achieved!

Quantum supremacy, achieved?

The news recently was agog with the claim that the so-called and highly sought "quantum supremacy" had been achieved via an effort undertaken by Google researchers.

Not everyone agreed though that the Google effort warranted waving the superlative supremacy flag.

That's not to say that the use of their 54-qubit Sycamore processor wasn't notable, and in fact, does provide another handy stride toward achieving viable quantum computing, but whether it was the vaunted moment of true supreme magnificence is something that many would argue is premature and supremely debatable.

Let's first consider what the fuss about quantum computers consists of and then noodle on the supremacy claim.

*In addition, it would be useful to ponder how quantum computers will impact the advent of truly self-driving cars.*

## Quantum Computing Explained

Today, our conventional computers pretty much employ the same hardware architecture that they have since the beginning of the computer field.

Sure, the hardware has gotten faster, smaller, and cheaper in cost, yet nonetheless, the underlying design principles and operational approach is still intact.

Often referred to as classical computing, you can also be in-the-know by calling the hardware a Turing machine (named after Alan Turing, a pioneer in mathematics and computing), or at times mumble to your friends and everyday strangers that the hardware is von Neumann architecture (named after physicist and mathematician John von Neumann).

Now that you've gotten that groundwork, it is time to introduce Einstein into this equation.

In physics, there is a field of study known as quantum mechanics. At the atomic and subatomic level of our universe and matter, there are aspects going on that seem to be somewhat mysterious and not readily explained by ordinary physics. Those in the field of quantum mechanics offer indubitably fascinating theories to explain the unusual behaviors occurring at the particle and sub-particle levels.

For example, it appears that particles can be somehow connected with each other when at long distances from each other, and yet there's no apparent reason why the disparate particles should be able to interconnect with each other. Generally, this is known as quantum entanglement.

Einstein was in the middle of the heyday of quantum mechanics formulation. He is famously known for having said that this surprising kind of entanglement is "spooky action at a distance" and fretted over how such an odd phenomenon could be fully explained.

Thus, you can quote Einstein that this whole thing is spooky.

Anyway, the thing is, even if you do or don't buy into the competing theories, the phenomena itself do appear to exist and therefore we might as well exploit it.

For computers, it was thought that you could construct the bits and bytes, the memory components, utilizing the quantum approach, and potentially be able to dramatically speed-up the computer memory capability.

Since this is a different approach to conventional computers, it has become known as quantum computing, consisting of a special computer that leverages the quantum aspects and does so using what are called qubits. Qubits are like classical bits but are revved up on steroids so that they are essentially faster, much faster than today's conventional computers.

Right now, it is extremely expensive to build a quantum computer, and it is relatively large, and it requires immense cooling, and it has just a few of the qubits thus it isn't yet anywhere near to its full potential, etc.

Of course, you can't go around saying that computers are too big and bulky, which some said during the era of vacuum tubes and predicted that computers would always need an entire room of space, yet today we have smartphones in our pockets that are many times more powerful than the early mainframes.

It is reasonable to assume that quantum computers will ultimately get smaller, more robust, less costly, and so on, though it is going to be many years, likely decades, before that happens, if it can happen at all.

You might be wondering what a quantum computer can do for you that a classical computer cannot do.

Why care about all this chatter about quantum this or that?

Well, in theory, a quantum computer can be vastly faster at computational efforts than can a classical computer. We're talking extraordinarily super-duper faster.

One area that this faster speed is stoking concern involves the use of encryption that we have in our digital world to protect our text messages and our files stored on faraway disk drives.

Most people assume that encryption is impossible to crack without having the secret key.

Most of today's encryption algorithms rely on the aspect that to crack contemporary encryption would require a tremendous amount of computing power and therefore is computationally expensive or nearly intractable.

If it took the fastest conventional computer say 10,000 years to crack your encrypted files, you could suggest that for all practical purposes the encryption was uncrackable, even though the truth is that it could be cracked if you were willing to wait those ten thousand years while a computer is humming away at doing so.

Via a quantum computer, you might be able to crack an encrypted file in months, or maybe just days, or perhaps even in minutes, depending upon the type of encryption used and the size or capability of the quantum computer.

This is scary since it means that someone grabbing up encrypted files of today might sit on those files and wait until quantum computers get better situated, and then decide to crack the files and see what secrets were being hidden away at that earlier time.

The other side to that coin is that we can shift toward stronger encryption with classical computers, and likely exploit quantum computers toward forging tougher encryption schemes.

Quantum computing is one of the hottest trending fields and will continue ahead with great fanfare.

Open questions abound such as whether there are classes of problems that can be solved by quantum computers that cannot be solved at all by classical computers, meaning that other than speed alone, perhaps there are types of problems we've never touched or thought to solve with classical that could be shorn with quantum.

One debate too is whether there are problems that classical computers can solve that perhaps a quantum computer cannot solve or that the quantum world does worse in trying to solve in comparison to a conventional computer.

This leads us to the quantum supremacy topic.

When you get various learned computer people into a room and they have different ideas about how to do things, invariably they form into opposing camps. One camp will claim that they have a better approach, while the other camp will refute the claim.

It's like rooting for your favorite football team or preferred brand of whiskey.

Those in the quantum computer camp had proposed that someday there would be an indication that a quantum computer could outdo a classical computer. When that day arrived, it would showcase the supremacy of quantum computers, ergo, the infamous slogan of quantum supremacy.

Google alleged that their recent effort met the quantum supremacy goal and that the task they performed with their experimental quantum computer would have taken 10,000 years for a conventional computer, but others disagreed and asserted that a classical computer could perform the same task in about 2-3 days.

One can understand the intense desire to raise the quantum supremacy flag by those that are squarely in the quantum camp, though the goalposts for measuring "supremacy" are somewhat ill-defined or some argue poorly defined (there are disputes as to what metrics to use), and some believed it was jumping the gun to make such a bold proclamation.

Also, if you look at the zillions of problems being solved today by conventional or classical computers, those problems are not yet able to be solved by the quantum computers still being formulated in R&D mode.

Is it fair or reasonable to say that quantum is supreme when it is still far less capable than today's everyday computing across-the-board?

Tilting the acrimony on its head, perhaps this argument about supremacy is lacking in civility anyway, and unbecoming, one might argue.

Yes, the supremacy crown is a means to spur development toward quantum computers, and yes, the esprit de corps perhaps gets the creative juices flowing and can attract public attention, but in the end, hopefully, we view computers as a tool and one that all of us ought to be finding ways to further extend and advance.

I'm sure that I'll be getting dinged by both camps in my efforts to amend the potential polarization on this topic, which is par for the course these days (sadness).

Let's shift our attention to true self-driving cars and how they will be impacted by the advent of quantum computers.

## The Levels Of Self-Driving Cars

It is important to clarify what I mean when referring to true self-driving cars.

True self-driving cars are ones that the AI drives the car entirely on its own and there isn't any human assistance during the driving task.

These driverless cars are considered a Level 4 and Level 5, while a car that requires a human driver to co-share the driving effort is usually considered at a Level 2 or Level 3. The cars that co-share the driving task are described as being semi-autonomous, and typically contain a variety of automated add-ons that are referred to as ADAS (Advanced Driver-Assistance Systems).

There is not yet a true self-driving car at Level 5, which we don't yet even know if this will be possible to achieve, and nor how long it will take to get there.

Meanwhile, the Level 4 efforts are gradually trying to get some traction by undergoing very narrow and selective public roadway trials, though there is controversy over whether this testing should be allowed per se (we are all life-or-death guinea pigs in an experiment taking place on our highways and byways, some point out).

Since semi-autonomous cars require a human driver, such cars aren't particularly going to be different per se than conventional cars when it comes to the quantum topic.

It is notable to point out that in spite of those dolts that keep posting videos of themselves falling asleep at the wheel of a Level 2 or Level 3 car, do not be misled into believing that you can take away your attention from the driving task while driving a semi-autonomous car.

You are the responsible party for the driving actions of the car, regardless of how much automation might be tossed into a Level 2 or Level 3.

## Self-Driving Cars And Quantum Computers

For Level 4 and Level 5 true self-driving cars, quantum computers can be a handy aid.

First, let's put aside the near-term chances of quantum computers becoming small enough, cheap enough, and otherwise be amendable to being used in a car as an onboard form of computer processing.

I'm knocking that out of the running for now.

Way beyond the near-term it might be feasible to have on-board quantum computers, but don't hold your breath for it to happen.

Does that toss out quantum computers from being useful for self-driving cars?

Heck, no!

Keep in mind that self-driving cars will have OTA (Over-The-Air) electronic communications capabilities, doing so to grab system updates for the on-board AI system from the cloud, and to push data collected by the self-driving car up to the cloud.

Quantum computers could have a welcoming spot in the cloud for the aiding of true self-driving cars.

This is not some far off futuristic notion since today there are already cloud-based quantum computer resources available, for which researchers and others are playing with online.

Indeed, I've done quantum computing programming via the cloud, and it is a blast, plus it highlights that we are all still figuring out what kind of specialized programming languages ought to be used, and what kinds of specialized database-like structures should be used for quantum computing.

One caution to keep in mind is that today's early versions of quantum computing are often fraught with high error rates. The exploration of how to contend with and mitigate or reduce system error rates in the qubits is an ongoing focus of inquiry (typically known as the quantum noise problem).

Overall, an in-the-cloud quantum computer (preferably not a simulation of one), could be used in a myriad of ways to help self-driving cars.

For example, the AI system that's on-board the self-driving car is fed updates from time-to-time that are based on analyses of the roadway data being collected. Via forms of Machine Learning (ML) and Deep Learning (DL), the AI system is enhanced while sitting in the cloud, tested on simulated roadway data, and then when readied it is pushed out into the driverless cars for in-car use.

The computational effort of the ML/DL while in the cloud can be huge, consuming tons and tons of classical computing cycles. This means that it can take a while to craft new updates for the on-board AI system, plus it can be quite costly to chew-up all those conventional computer cycles.

Into the picture steps quantum computers.

You could have a quantum computer in the cloud that participates in the AI enhancing task, and because of the tremendous speed advantages (possibly), you might be able to generate a revised AI that can be sooner pushed out to the driverless cars in a fleet.

Think of it this way.

Suppose some driverless cars happened upon an edge or corner case of some roadway instance, one that hadn't been earlier experienced by any of the self-driving cars in a fleet. This data might be pushed up to the cloud, crunched right away, and a new update flashed out to the driverless cars, quickly getting them all up-to-speed based on the latest learned element from other fellow self-driving cars.

I'm not suggesting that the quantum computer did something new, and instead of saying that we can exploit its speediness as part of the updating efforts for the driverless cars in the field.

If done properly, it means that those driverless cars are better off sooner, meaning that human passengers are better off sooner, and likewise anyone that comes near to a driverless car is presumably better off since the self-driving car has gotten an enhancement.

Don't misinterpret this to suggest that the quantum approach is a panacea.

There could, unfortunately, be a temptation to also use the speediness to inadvertently cut corners and push out some update that isn't ready for prime time.

Hopefully, the self-driving tech makers and those leveraging the cloud capabilities involving quantum will be as steady and somber with quantum computers as they would with everyday conventional computing.

### Conclusion

Another facet of utilizing quantum computers while in-the-cloud would be to use them for doing the scheduling of car traffic and undertaking traffic management.

Some believe that once we have a prevalence of driverless cars, they could interact and coordinate to reduce traffic congestion.

Besides electronically communicating with each other via V2V (vehicle-to-vehicle) electronic communication, and via V2I (vehicle-to-infrastructure) communication, they might also interact with a "master" traffic management system that is trying to even out the flow of thousands of cars on the roadways.

The computational effort to do traffic management can be quite overbearing, so the speed of quantum computers in-the-cloud might aid such an effort.

I realize that some of you might be wondering whether the quantum computer could be fast enough that even though it is sitting in the cloud that it could nonetheless become the driver of a self-driving car.

I vote no.

As per my earlier posting that covers the dangers of using wireless as a driving approach, the risks associated with the driver being remote, whether a human remote driver or a quantum computer remotely driving, does not bode well for the safety of self-driving cars.

That being said, the onboard AI could certainly consult with the quantum computer in the cloud, doing so to get an added "opinion" about a driving matter, though this would need to be done under the expectation that there is a latency of getting a result from the cloud (or, no answer at all due to the cloud connection being untenable).

Quantum computers will be a vital addition to the portfolio of computing capabilities.

The field of quantum computing is still in its infancy.

I hope that this discussion has prompted you to become a *quantum conversant* (an "in" term for becoming familiar with quantum computing).

I encourage anyone that is eager to contribute toward the future of computers to consider getting involved in or becoming more aware of quantum computing.

I ask just one small promise.

Keep the supremacy clamoring to a modest level and do not go around wearing those Quantum Supremacy blaring T-shirts unless you are also willing to include Classical Supremacy on the same shirt with the same boldness and earnestness.

Just aiming for world peace, thanks.

# CHAPTER 12

# RELIGIOUS REVIVAL

# AND

# AI SELF-DRIVING CARS

# CHAPTER 12

# RELIGIOUS REVIVAL

# AND

# AI SELF-DRIVING CARS

Nationwide statistics indicate that Americans are becoming less affiliated with established religions.

Over one-third currently say that they are not affiliated with any religion, which is a doubling in number since about a decade ago.

There are numerous theories about why there is this dropping level of affiliation, a precipitous drop that bodes alarming concerns for those that embrace religious efforts and support.

Here are some of the voiced reasons that the U.S. is seemingly drifting away from religions:

- Lack of social impetus toward adopting religious beliefs
- Social pressures to overtly avoid having religious affiliations
- Parents that have muted religious beliefs and therefore do not pass them along
- Family life that is relatively devoid of religious interest
- Rise of alt-religious efforts that become pseudo substitutes
- Qualms about differences in opinion on matters of gender, sex, and other factors
- Perceived conflict in personal politics views versus political positions by religions
- Unconformable with tension between religions and scientific disciplines
- Etc.

One argument being made is that young Americans have a flawed and incomplete understanding of what religions are and what they stand for.

It has been suggested that many of the aforementioned concerns about religion could be dissuaded if the youth of the country were properly informed about today's religions and religious options open to them. Presumably, by having greater and easier access to religious teachings and information, young Americans would have a fuller picture and be more likely to, therefore, join and participate in established religions.

Here's an interesting question: *Could true self-driving cars be a spark that causes a revival in religious interests by young Americans?*

It might not be readily apparent at first glance as to how self-driving cars could somehow be a means or mechanism to rejuvenate religious interest per se, and indeed the two topics probably seem quite unrelated.

Let's unpack the matter and see.

### The Levels Of Self-Driving Cars

It is important to clarify what I mean when referring to true self-driving cars.

True self-driving cars are ones that the AI drives the car entirely on its own and there isn't any human assistance during the driving task.

These driverless cars are considered a Level 4 and Level 5, while a car that requires a human driver to co-share the driving effort is usually considered at a Level 2 or Level 3. The cars that co-share the driving task are described as being semi-autonomous, and typically contain a variety of automated add-ons that are referred to as ADAS (Advanced Driver-Assistance Systems).

There is not yet a true self-driving car at Level 5, which we don't yet even know if this will be possible to achieve, and nor how long it will take to get there.

Meanwhile, the Level 4 efforts are gradually trying to get some traction by undergoing very narrow and selective public roadway trials, though there is controversy over whether this testing should be allowed per se (we are all life-or-death guinea pigs in an experiment taking place on our highways and byways, some point out).

Since semi-autonomous cars require a human driver, such cars will not be a nudge or catalyst toward a religious revival any more than are today's conventional cars.

It is notable to point out that in spite of those human drivers that keep posting videos of themselves falling asleep at the wheel of a Level 2 or Level 3 car, do not be misled into believing that you can take away your attention from the driving task while driving a semi-autonomous car.

You are the responsible party for the driving actions of the car, regardless of how much automation might be tossed into a Level 2 or Level 3.

## Self-Driving Cars And Religious Info Access

For Level 4 and Level 5 true self-driving cars, it might be prudent to consider how there might be a spark to ignite renewed interest in religions.

First, let's put aside a somewhat outstretched reason that some have floated, namely that the advent of cars that drive themselves might be an amazement to the public and thusly bring forth notions of being able to go beyond the realm of human reasoning.

Contemporary folks aren't going to be shocked or seeking extraordinary explanations to comprehend the advent of driverless cars.

In short, there isn't going to be any kind of revelation that alters people's perception of the world simply due to the emergence of self-driving cars. Sure, maybe if you introduced a driverless car during the days of the horse and buggy, and suddenly had a driverless car that miraculously appeared in the middle of a stone age like era, you'd get quite a few converts toward seeking alternative explanations.

For today's smartphone totting public, we all know today that driverless cars are still just bits and bytes.

There isn't any true human thinking form of intelligence embodied in these AI systems, indeed such systems lack any kind of common-sense reasoning, and there is most definitely not a recreation of sentient capabilities into the car's onboard hardware and software.

The key to arguing that self-driving cars might spur religious interest and affiliation is found in a much more mundane and seemingly obvious but oft unstated reason.

It has to do with time and access.

Via driverless cars, most pundits predict that we will all be likely to travel in cars more so than we do today. Furthermore, we will all be passengers and not be drivers, since the AI system will be doing the driving for us.

Right now, there are an estimated 70 billion hours being used by Americans as they drive their cars, doing so to get to work or driving to do errands. Those billions of hours are today consumed with a focus on driving a car. With self-driving cars, those billions of hours can be put toward some other use.

One such use would be for Americans to potentially become more versed in religions and have greater access and time available to engage in religious learnings.

If the point about young Americans having a flawed understanding about religions is the cornerstone of decreases in religious affiliations, perhaps the emergence of self-driving cars would give those young Americans the needed time and access to religious info that would bring them back into the fold.

Here's how that could happen.

While inside a driverless car, you'll have nothing to do since you aren't tasked with driving the car.

Self-driving cars are going to be hooked up to wireless communications providing high-speed broadband Internet access during your car travels.

So, imagine that there will be hundreds of millions of Americans, all sitting in these driverless cars, and having nothing to do while going from place to place and that they will be in such cars a lot more than even the vast amount of time being spent in cars today.

This is a ripe and alluring chance to get out a message of one kind or another. There is a captive audience, likely eager to do something other than doing nothing while riding in a self-driving car.

Why not stream out religious teachings?

Why not setup interactive sessions allowing those in a driverless car in Iowa to discuss religious topics with people in a self-driving car in California or Oregon?

The ease of being able to broadcast religious info will be multiplied tremendously.

And, beyond just pushing out content, there will be interactivity readily available too.

Within a self-driving car, there is bound to be a camera pointing inward, normally being used to make sure that someone riding in a driverless car doesn't mar the interior with graffiti or tear-up the leather seats. That same camera can be used for interacting with others that might be anywhere, whether in another driverless car someplace or sitting at home or residing in a religious church.

Virtual religious groups could be formed on-the-fly.

There could be organized religious events that occur and are broadcast on a regular basis, perhaps timed with the morning commute or the evening ride home.

Overall, the advent of self-driving cars opens a whole new door into having access to Americans and leveraging their otherwise unused time while inside a driverless car.

### Physical Access To Religious Aspects Too

Let's double-down on the matter.

In addition to leveraging the digital approach, there is also the opportunity to make use of the expanded mobility capabilities due to driverless cars.

There are people today that might be mobility disadvantaged and cannot readily get over to a religious meeting. They lack a means of mobility that can get them to where they'd like to go.

It is believed that self-driving cars are going to broaden mobility, making the act of getting from point A to point B much easier, perhaps nearly becoming friction-free in terms of today's mobility barriers and hurdles.

Someone that hasn't been to church in years could find that they can now easily get there by making use of a ride-sharing driverless car.

Indeed, a religious entity might arrange with a driverless car ridesharing service to go around and pick-up people that are interested in attending a religious event or rally, and readily give those interested parties a free lift to the locale (the cost covered by the religious entity).

Thinking even further out-of-the-box, perhaps some religious entities might decide to buy or lease a fleet of self-driving cars, allowing the religion to use driverless cars as needed and when so desired.

In addition to transporting people to a religious event, it would be feasible to have religious teachers that go to see someone that might be interested in knowing more about religion.

Getting religious teachers to someone's home or other location could be eased using self-driving cars. Those religious teachers don't need to know how to drive and aren't burdened with the driving task, plus there's no logistical difficulties associated with having to find a driver.

There could also be religious teachers that are ride-a-long available.

Maybe on Friday mornings, while heading to work, a pre-arranged effort takes place as you and some neighbors jump into a driverless car, and then pick-up a religious teacher on the way. During the driving journey, a lively discussion takes place on some religious topics of mutual interest.

## Conclusion

Though the driverless car certainly appears to be a likely spark for religion interest, we need to keep in mind that self-driving cars can be put toward many other activities and thus it is not necessarily going to be used exclusively or entirely for religious-related matters.

Some predict that we are going to have a massive rise in online game playing, occurring as a result of driverless cars. Namely, people will use the time inside a driverless car to play their favorite online game.

If you are already wringing your hands that young Americans spend too much time playing online games, you'd better steady yourself for what might happen in the future.

In lieu of playing games, one can watch a movie or a favored TV show, streamed live or recorded, using up the time while on a driverless car journey.

What about sleep?

Those kids of yours that did their late-night homework and were exhausted by their extracurricular activities might decide to take a nap in the driverless car, doing so while heading to school or after school and heading to yet another activity.

Just because the time and access are going to be made available, it doesn't ergo mean that for sure there will be religious matters that fill the void.

Inevitably, there is going to be some amount of driverless car usage that involves religions, since self-driving cars open the possibility of expanding the reach of religious teachings. How much and in what manner is something yet to be ascertained.

Some will relish these possibilities; others might find them of concern.

Whichever viewpoint you might have on the matter, the overarching point is that society can potentially be transformed in many ways as a result of the advent of self-driving cars, and we ought to be thinking seriously about how it will play out.

Better now than later.

# APPENDIX

# APPENDIX A
# TEACHING WITH THIS MATERIAL

The material in this book can be readily used either as a supplemental to other content for a class, or it can also be used as a core set of textbook material for a specialized class. Classes where this material is most likely used include any classes at the college or university level that want to augment the class by offering thought provoking and educational essays about AI and self-driving cars.

In particular, here are some aspects for class use:

o   Computer Science. Studying AI, autonomous vehicles, etc.

o   Business. Exploring technology and it adoption for business.

o   Sociology. Sociological views on the adoption and advancement of technology.

Specialized classes at the undergraduate and graduate level can also make use of this material.

For each chapter, consider whether you think the chapter provides material relevant to your course topic. There is plenty of opportunity to get the students thinking about the topic and force them to decide whether they agree or disagree with the points offered and positions taken. I would also encourage you to have the students do additional research beyond the chapter material presented (I provide next some suggested assignments they can do).

# RESEARCH ASSIGNMENTS ON THESE TOPICS

Your students can find background material on these topics, doing so in various business and technical publications. I list below the top ranked AI related journals. For business publications, I would suggest the usual culprits such as the Harvard Business Review, Forbes, Fortune, WSJ, and the like.

Here are some suggestions of homework or projects that you could assign to students:

a) Assignment for foundational AI research topic: Research and prepare a paper and a presentation on a specific aspect of Deep AI, Machine Learning, ANN, etc. The paper should cite at least 3 reputable sources. Compare and contrast to what has been stated in this book.

b) Assignment for the Self-Driving Car topic: Research and prepare a paper and Self-Driving Cars. Cite at least 3 reputable sources and analyze the characterizations. Compare and contrast to what has been stated in this book.

c) Assignment for a Business topic: Research and prepare a paper and a presentation on businesses and advanced technology. What is hot, and what is not? Cite at least 3 reputable sources. Compare and contrast to the depictions in this book.

d) Assignment to do a Startup: Have the students prepare a paper about how they might startup a business in this realm. They must submit a sound Business Plan for the startup. They could also be asked to present their Business Plan and so should also have a presentation deck to coincide with it.

You can certainly adjust the aforementioned assignments to fit to your particular needs and the class structure. You'll notice that I ask for 3 reputable cited sources for the paper writing based assignments. I usually steer students toward "reputable" publications, since otherwise they will cite some oddball source that has no credentials other than that they happened to write something and post it onto the Internet. You can define "reputable" in whatever way you prefer, for example some faculty think Wikipedia is not reputable while others believe it is reputable and allow students to cite it.

The reason that I usually ask for at least 3 citations is that if the student only does one or two citations they usually settle on whatever they happened to find the fastest. By requiring three citations, it usually seems to force them to look around, explore, and end-up probably finding five or more, and then whittling it down to 3 that they will actually use.

I have not specified the length of their papers, and leave that to you to tell the students what you prefer. For each of those assignments, you could end-up with a short one to two pager, or you could do a dissertation length paper. Base the length on whatever best fits for your class, and the credit amount of the assignment within the context of the other grading metrics you'll be using for the class.

I mention in the assignments that they are to do a paper and prepare a presentation. I usually try to get students to present their work. This is a good practice for what they will do in the business world. Most of the time, they will be required to prepare an analysis and present it. If you don't have the class time or inclination to have the students present, then you can of course cut out the aspect of them putting together a presentation.

If you want to point students toward highly ranked journals in AI, here's a list of the top journals as reported by *various citation counts sources* (this list changes year to year):

- o   Communications of the ACM
- o   Artificial Intelligence
- o   Cognitive Science
- o   IEEE Transactions on Pattern Analysis and Machine Intelligence
- o   Foundations and Trends in Machine Learning
- o   Journal of Memory and Language
- o   Cognitive Psychology
- o   Neural Networks
- o   IEEE Transactions on Neural Networks and Learning Systems
- o   IEEE Intelligent Systems
- o   Knowledge-based Systems

# GUIDE TO USING THE CHAPTERS

For each of the chapters, I provide next some various ways to use the chapter material. You can assign the tasks as individual homework assignments, or the tasks can be used with team projects for the class. You can easily layout a series of assignments, such as indicating that the students are to do item "a" below for say Chapter 1, then "b" for the next chapter of the book, and so on.

a) What is the main point of the chapter and describe in your own words the significance of the topic,

b) Identify at least two aspects in the chapter that you agree with, and support your concurrence by providing at least one other outside researched item as support; make sure to explain your basis for disagreeing with the aspects,

c) Identify at least two aspects in the chapter that you disagree with, and support your disagreement by providing at least one other outside researched item as support; make sure to explain your basis for disagreeing with the aspects,

d) Find an aspect that was not covered in the chapter, doing so by conducting outside research, and then explain how that aspect ties into the chapter and what significance it brings to the topic,

e) Interview a specialist in industry about the topic of the chapter, collect from them their thoughts and opinions, and readdress the chapter by citing your source and how they compared and contrasted to the material,

f) Interview a relevant academic professor or researcher in a college or university about the topic of the chapter, collect from them their thoughts and opinions, and readdress the chapter by citing your source and how they compared and contrasted to the material,

g) Try to update a chapter by finding out the latest on the topic, and ascertain whether the issue or topic has now been solved or whether it is still being addressed, explain what you come up with.

The above are all ways in which you can get the students of your class involved in considering the material of a given chapter. You could mix things up by having one of those above assignments per each week, covering the chapters over the course of the semester or quarter.

As a reminder, here are the chapters of the book and you can select whichever chapters you find most valued for your particular class:

### Chapter Title

1   Eliot Framework for AI Self-Driving Cars

2   Germs Spreading and AI Self-Driving Cars

3   Carbon Footprint and AI Self-Driving Cars

4   Protestors Use Of AI Self-Driving Cars

5   Rogue Behavior and AI Self-Driving Cars

6   Using Human Drivers Versus AI Self-Driving Cars

7   Tesla Hodge-Podge On AI Self-Driving Cars

8   Solo Occupancy and AI Self-Driving Cars

9   Einstein's Twins Paradox and AI Self-Driving Cars

10   Nation-State Takeover Of AI Self-Driving Cars

11   Quantum Computers and AI Self-Driving Cars

12   Religious Revival And AI Self-Driving Cars

Companion Book By This Author

### *Advances in AI and Autonomous Vehicles: Cybernetic Self-Driving Cars*

*Practical Advances in Artificial Intelligence (AI) and Machine Learning*

by

## Dr. Lance B. Eliot, MBA, PhD

Chapter Title

1   Genetic Algorithms for Self-Driving Cars

2   Blockchain for Self-Driving Cars

3   Machine Learning and Data for Self-Driving Cars

4   Edge Problems at Core of True Self-Driving Cars

5   Solving the Roundabout Traversal Problem for SD Cars

6   Parallel Parking Mindless Task for SD Cars: Step It Up

7   Caveats of Open Source for Self-Driving Cars

8   Catastrophic Cyber Hacking of Self-Driving Cars

9   Conspicuity for Self-Driving Cars

10  Accident Scene Traversal for Self-Driving Cars

11  Emergency Vehicle Awareness for Self-Driving Cars

12  Are Left Turns Right for Self-Driving Cars

13  Going Blind: When Sensors Fail on Self-Driving Cars

14  Roadway Debris Cognition for Self-Driving Cars

15  Avoiding Pedestrian Roadkill by Self-Driving Cars

16  When Accidents Happen to Self-Driving Cars

17  Illegal Driving for Self-Driving Cars

18  Making AI Sense of Road Signs

19  Parking Your Car the AI Way

20  Not Fast Enough: Human Factors in Self-Driving Cars

21  State of Government Reporting on Self-Driving Cars

22  The Head Nod Problem for Self-Driving Cars

23  CES Reveals Self-Driving Car Differences

**This title is available via Amazon and other book sellers**

Companion Book By This Author

### *Self-Driving Cars:*
### *"The Mother of All AI Projects"*

by Dr. Lance B. Eliot, MBA, PhD

Chapter Title

1  Grand Convergence Explains Rise of Self-Driving Cars

2  Here is Why We Need to Call Them Self-Driving Cars

3  Richter Scale for Levels of Self-Driving Cars

4  LIDAR as Secret Sauce for Self-Driving Cars

5  Pied Piper Approach to SD Car-Following

6  Sizzle Reel Trickery for AI Self-Driving Car Hype

7  Roller Coaster Public Perception of Self-Driving Cars

8  Brainless Self-Driving Shuttles Not Same as SD Cars

9  First Salvo Class Action Lawsuits for Defective SD Cars

10  AI Fake News About Self-Driving Cars

11  Rancorous Ranking of Self-Driving Cars

12  Product Liability for Self-Driving Cars

13  Humans Colliding with Self-Driving Cars

14  Elderly Boon or Bust for Self-Driving Cars

15  Simulations for Self-Driving Cars: Machine Learning

16  DUI Drunk Driving by Self-Driving Cars

17  Ten Human-Driving Foibles: Deep Learning

18  Art of Defensive Driving is Key to Self-Driving Cars

19  Cyclops Approach to AI Self-Driving Cars is Myopic

20  Steering Wheel Gets Self-Driving Car Attention

21  Remote Piloting is a Self-Driving Car Crutch

22  Self-Driving Cars: Zero Fatalities, Zero Chance

23  Goldrush: Self-Driving Car Lawsuit Bonanza Ahead

24  Road Trip Trickery for Self-Driving Trucks and Cars

25  Ethically Ambiguous Self-Driving Car

*This title is available via Amazon and other book sellers*

Companion Book By This Author

## Innovation and Thought Leadership on Self-Driving Driverless Cars

by Dr. Lance B. Eliot, MBA, PhD

Chapter Title

1  Sensor Fusion for Self-Driving Cars

2  Street Scene Free Space Detection Self-Driving Cars

3  Self-Awareness for Self-Driving Cars

4  Cartographic Trade-offs for Self-Driving Cars

5  Toll Road Traversal for Self-Driving Cars

6  Predictive Scenario Modeling for Self-Driving Cars

7  Selfishness for Self-Driving Cars

8  Leap Frog Driving for Self-Driving Cars

9  Proprioceptive IMU's for Self-Driving Cars

10  Robojacking of Self-Driving Cars

11  Self-Driving Car Moonshot and Mother of AI Projects

12  Marketing of Self-Driving Cars

13  Are Airplane Autopilots Same as Self-Driving Cars

14  Savvy Self-Driving Car Regulators: Marc Berman

15  Event Data Recorders (EDR) for Self-Driving Cars

16  Looking Behind You for Self-Driving Cars

17  In-Car Voice Commands NLP for Self-Driving Cars

18  When Self-Driving Cars Get Pulled Over by a Cop

19  Brainjacking Neuroprosthetus Self-Driving Cars

**This title is available via Amazon and other book sellers**

Companion Book By This Author
## New Advances in AI Autonomous
## Driverless Cars Self-Driving Cars
by Dr. Lance B. Eliot, MBA, PhD

Chapter Title

1   Eliot Framework for AI Self-Driving Cars

2   Self-Driving Cars Learning from Self-Driving Cars

3   Imitation as Deep Learning for Self-Driving Cars

4   Assessing Federal Regulations for Self-Driving Cars

5   Bandwagon Effect for Self-Driving Cars

6   AI Backdoor Security Holes for Self-Driving Cars

7   Debiasing of AI for Self-Driving Cars

8   Algorithmic Transparency for Self-Driving Cars

9   Motorcycle Disentanglement for Self-Driving Cars

10  Graceful Degradation Handling of Self-Driving Cars

11  AI for Home Garage Parking of Self-Driving Cars

12  Motivational AI Irrationality for Self-Driving Cars

13  Curiosity as Cognition for Self-Driving Cars

14  Automotive Recalls of Self-Driving Cars

15  Internationalizing AI for Self-Driving Cars

16  Sleeping as AI Mechanism for Self-Driving Cars

17  Car Insurance Scams and Self-Driving Cars

18  U-Turn Traversal AI for Self-Driving Cars

19  Software Neglect for Self-Driving Cars

*This title is available via Amazon and other book sellers*

Companion Book By This Author

## Introduction to
## Driverless Self-Driving Cars

by Dr. Lance B. Eliot, MBA, PhD

Chapter Title

1 Self-Driving Car Moonshot: Mother of All AI Projects
2 Grand Convergence Leads to Self-Driving Cars
3 Why They Should Be Called Self-Driving Cars
4 Richter Scale for Self-Driving Car Levels
5 LIDAR for Self-Driving Cars
6 Overall Framework for Self-Driving Cars
7 Sensor Fusion is Key for Self-Driving Cars
8 Humans Not Fast Enough for Self-Driving Cars
9 Solving Edge Problems of Self-Driving Cars
10 Graceful Degradation for Faltering Self-Driving Cars
11 Genetic Algorithms for Self-Driving Cars
12 Blockchain for Self-Driving Cars
13 Machine Learning and Data for Self-Driving Cars
14 Cyber-Hacking of Self-Driving Cars
15 Sensor Failures in Self-Driving Cars
16 When Accidents Happen to Self-Driving Cars
17 Backdoor Security Holes in Self-Driving Cars
18 Future Brainjacking for Self-Driving Cars
19 Internationalizing Self-Driving Cars
20 Are Airline Autopilots Same as Self-Driving Cars
21 Marketing of Self-Driving Cars
22 Fake News about Self-Driving Cars
23 Product Liability for Self-Driving Cars
24 Zero Fatalities Zero Chance for Self-Driving Cars
25 Road Trip Trickery for Self-Driving Cars
26 Ethical Issues of Self-Driving Cars
27 Ranking of Self-Driving Cars
28 Induced Demand Driven by Self-Driving Cars

**This title is available via Amazon and other book sellers**

Companion Book By This Author

### *Autonomous Vehicle Driverless*
### *Self-Driving Cars and Artificial Intelligence*

by Dr. Lance B. Eliot, MBA, PhD

Chapter Title

1  Eliot Framework for AI Self-Driving Cars

2  Rocket Man Drivers and AI Self-Driving Cars

3  Occam's Razor Crucial for AI Self-Driving Cars

4  Simultaneous Local/Map (SLAM) for Self-Driving Cars

5  Swarm Intelligence for AI Self-Driving Cars

6  Biomimicry and Robomimicry for Self-Driving Cars

7  Deep Compression/Pruning for AI Self-Driving Cars

8  Extra-Scenery Perception for AI Self-Driving Cars

9  Invasive Curve and AI Self-Driving Cars

10  Normalization of Deviance and AI Self-Driving Cars

11  Groupthink Dilemma for AI Self-Driving Cars

12  Induced Demand Driven by AI Self-Driving Cars

13  Compressive Sensing for AI Self-Driving Cars

14  Neural Layer Explanations for AI Self-Driving Cars

15  Self-Adapting Resiliency for AI Self-Driving Cars

16  Prisoner's Dilemma and AI Self-Driving Cars

17  Turing Test and AI Self-Driving Cars

18  Support Vector Machines for AI Self-Driving Cars

19  "Expert Systems and AI Self-Driving Cars" by Michael Eliot

**This title is available via Amazon and other book sellers**

Companion Book By This Author

## *Transformative Artificial Intelligence*
## *Driverless Self-Driving Cars*

by Dr. Lance B. Eliot, MBA, PhD

Chapter Title

1   Eliot Framework for AI Self-Driving Cars

2   Kinetosis Anti-Motion Sickness for Self-Driving Cars

3   Rain Driving for Self-Driving Cars

4   Edge Computing for Self-Driving Cars

5   Motorcycles as AI Self-Driving Vehicles

6   CAPTCHA Cyber-Hacking and Self-Driving Cars

7   Probabilistic Reasoning for Self-Driving Cars

8   Proving Grounds for Self-Driving Cars

9   Frankenstein and AI Self-Driving Cars

10  Omnipresence for Self-Driving Cars

11  Looking Behind You for Self-Driving Cars

12  Over-The-Air (OTA) Updating for Self-Driving Cars

13  Snow Driving for Self-Driving Cars

14  Human-Aided Training for Self-Driving Cars

15  Privacy for Self-Driving Cars

16  Transduction Vulnerabilities for Self-Driving Cars

17  Conversations Computing and Self-Driving Cars

18  Flying Debris and Self-Driving Cars

19  Citizen AI for Self-Driving Cars

*This title is available via Amazon and other book sellers*

<u>Companion Book By This Author</u>

### *Disruptive Artificial Intelligence and Driverless Self-Driving Cars*

by Dr. Lance B. Eliot, MBA, PhD

<u>Chapter Title</u>

1  Eliot Framework for AI Self-Driving Cars

2  Maneuverability and Self-Driving Cars

3  Common Sense Reasoning and Self-Driving Cars

4  Cognition Timing and Self-Driving Cars

5  Speed Limits and Self-Driving Vehicles

6  Human Back-up Drivers and Self-Driving Cars

7  Forensic Analysis Uber and Self-Driving Cars

8  Power Consumption and Self-Driving Cars

9  Road Rage and Self-Driving Cars

10  Conspiracy Theories and Self-Driving Cars

11  Fear Landscape and Self-Driving Cars

12  Pre-Mortem and Self-Driving Cars

13  Kits and Self-Driving Cars

*This title is available via Amazon and other book sellers*

Companion Book By This Author

### *State-of-the-Art*
### *AI Driverless Self-Driving Cars*

by Dr. Lance B. Eliot, MBA, PhD

Chapter Title

1   Eliot Framework for AI Self-Driving Cars

2   Versioning and Self-Driving Cars

3   Towing and Self-Driving Cars

4   Driving Styles and Self-Driving Cars

5   Bicyclists and Self-Driving Vehicles

6   Back-up Cams and Self-Driving Cars

7   Traffic Mix and Self-Driving Cars

8   Hot-Car Deaths and Self-Driving Cars

9   Machine Learning Performance and Self-Driving Cars

10  Sensory Illusions and Self-Driving Cars

11  Federated Machine Learning and Self-Driving Cars

12  Irreproducibility and Self-Driving Cars

13  In-Car Deliveries and Self-Driving Cars

*This title is available via Amazon and other book sellers*

Companion Book By This Author

### Top Trends in
### AI Self-Driving Cars

by Dr. Lance B. Eliot, MBA, PhD

Chapter Title

1  Eliot Framework for AI Self-Driving Cars

2  Responsibility and Self-Driving Cars

3  Changing Lanes and Self-Driving Cars

4  Procrastination and Self-Driving Cars

5  NTSB Report and Tesla Car Crash

6  Start Over AI and Self-Driving Cars

7  Freezing Robot Problem and Self-Driving Cars

8  Canarying and Self-Driving Cars

9  Nighttime Driving and Self-Driving Cars

10  Zombie-Cars Taxes and Self-Driving Cars

11  Traffic Lights and Self-Driving Cars

12  Reverse Engineering and Self-Driving Cars

13  Singularity AI and Self-Driving Cars

*This title is available via Amazon and other book sellers*

Companion Book By This Author

## *AI Innovations and Self-Driving Cars*

by Dr. Lance B. Eliot, MBA, PhD

Chapter Title

1   Eliot Framework for AI Self-Driving Cars

2   API's and Self-Driving Cars

3   Egocentric Designs and Self-Driving Cars

4   Family Road Trip and Self-Driving Cars

5   AI Developer Burnout and Tesla Car Crash

6   Stealing Secrets About Self-Driving Cars

7   Affordability and Self-Driving Cars

8   Crossing the Rubicon and Self-Driving Cars

9   Addicted to Self-Driving Cars

10   Ultrasonic Harm and Self-Driving Cars

11   Accidents Contagion and Self-Driving Cars

12   Non-Stop 24x7 and Self-Driving Cars

13   Human Life Spans and Self-Driving Cars

*This title is available via Amazon and other book sellers*

Companion Book By This Author

### *Crucial Advances for*
### *AI Self-Driving Cars*

by Dr. Lance B. Eliot, MBA, PhD

<u>Chapter Title</u>

1   Eliot Framework for AI Self-Driving Cars

2   Ensemble Learning and AI Self-Driving Cars

3   Ghost in AI Self-Driving Cars

4   Public Shaming of AI Self-Driving

5   Internet of Things (IoT) and AI Self-Driving Cars

6   Personal Rapid Transit (RPT) and Self-Driving Cars

7   Eventual Consistency and AI Self-Driving Cars

8   Mass Transit Future and AI Self-Driving Cars

9   Coopetition and AI Self-Driving Cars

10   Electric Vehicles (EVs) and AI Self-Driving Cars

11   Dangers of In-Motion AI Self-Driving Cars

12   Sports Cars and AI Self-Driving Cars

13   Game Theory and AI Self-Driving Cars

*This title is available via Amazon and other book sellers*

Companion Book By This Author

## *Sociotechnical Insights and AI Driverless Cars*

by Dr. Lance B. Eliot, MBA, PhD

Chapter Title

1   Eliot Framework for AI Self-Driving Cars

2   Start-ups and AI Self-Driving Cars

3   Code Obfuscation and AI Self-Driving Cars

4   Hyperlanes and AI Self-Driving Cars

5   Passenger Panic Inside an AI Self-Driving Car

6   Tech Stockholm Syndrome and Self-Driving Cars

7   Paralysis and AI Self-Driving Cars

8   Ugly Zones and AI Self-Driving Cars

9   Ridesharing and AI Self-Driving Cars

10  Multi-Party Privacy and AI Self-Driving Cars

11  Chaff Bugs and AI Self-Driving Cars

12  Social Reciprocity and AI Self-Driving Cars

13  Pet Mode and AI Self-Driving Cars

*This title is available via Amazon and other book sellers*

Companion Book By This Author

## *Pioneering Advances for AI Driverless Cars*

by Dr. Lance B. Eliot, MBA, PhD

Chapter Title

1 Eliot Framework for AI Self-Driving Cars

2 Boxes on Wheels and AI Self-Driving Cars

3 Clogs and AI Self-Driving Cars

4 Kids Communicating with AI Self-Driving Cars

5 Incident Awareness and AI Self-Driving Car

6 Emotion Recognition and Self-Driving Cars

7 Rear-End Collisions and AI Self-Driving Cars

8 Autonomous Nervous System and AI Self-Driving Cars

9 Height Warnings and AI Self-Driving Cars

10 Future Jobs and AI Self-Driving Cars

11 Car Wash and AI Self-Driving Cars

12 5G and AI Self-Driving Cars

13 Gen Z and AI Self-Driving Cars

*This title is available via Amazon and other book sellers*

Companion Book By This Author

*Leading Edge Trends for*
*AI Driverless Cars*

by Dr. Lance B. Eliot, MBA, PhD

Chapter Title

1   Eliot Framework for AI Self-Driving Cars

2   Pranking and AI Self-Driving Cars

3   Drive-Thrus and AI Self-Driving Cars

4   Overworking on AI Self-Driving Cars

5   Sleeping Barber Problem and AI Self-Driving Cars

6   System Load Balancing and AI Self-Driving Cars

7   Virtual Spike Strips and AI Self-Driving Cars

8   Razzle Dazzle Camouflage and AI Self-Driving Cars

9   Rewilding of AI Self-Driving Cars

10  Brute Force Algorithms and AI Self-Driving Cars

11  Idle Moments and AI Self-Driving Cars

12  Hurricanes and AI Self-Driving Cars

13  Object Visual Transplants and AI Self-Driving Cars

*This title is available via Amazon and other book sellers*

Companion Book By This Author

### *The Cutting Edge of AI Autonomous Cars*

by Dr. Lance B. Eliot, MBA, PhD

<u>Chapter Title</u>

1 Eliot Framework for AI Self-Driving Cars

2 Driving Controls and AI Self-Driving Cars

3 Bug Bounty and AI Self-Driving Cars

4 Lane Splitting and AI Self-Driving Cars

5 Drunk Drivers versus AI Self-Driving Cars

6 Internal Naysayers and AI Self-Driving Cars

7 Debugging and AI Self-Driving Cars

8 Ethics Review Boards and AI Self-Driving Cars

9 Road Diets and AI Self-Driving Cars

10 Wrong Way Driving and AI Self-Driving Cars

11 World Safety Summit and AI Self-Driving Cars

**This title is available via Amazon and other book sellers**

Companion Book By This Author

### The Next Wave of
### AI Self-Driving Cars

by Dr. Lance B. Eliot, MBA, PhD

Chapter Title

1   Eliot Framework for AI Self-Driving Cars

2   Productivity and AI Self-Driving Cars

3   Blind Pedestrians and AI Self-Driving Cars

4   Fail-Safe AI and AI Self-Driving Cars

5   Anomaly Detection and AI Self-Driving Cars

6   Running Out of Gas and AI Self-Driving Cars

7   Deep Personalization and AI Self-Driving Cars

8   Reframing the Levels of AI Self-Driving Cars

9   Cryptojacking and AI Self-Driving Cars

**This title is available via Amazon and other book sellers**

Companion Book By This Author

## *Revolutionary Innovations of AI Self-Driving Cars*

by Dr. Lance B. Eliot, MBA, PhD

Chapter Title

1   Eliot Framework for AI Self-Driving Cars

2   Exascale Supercomputer and AI Self-Driving Cars

3   Superhuman AI and AI Self-Driving Cars

4   Olfactory e-Nose Sensors and AI Self-Driving Cars

5   Perpetual Computing and AI Self-Driving Cars

6   Byzantine Generals Problem and AI Self-Driving Cars

7   Driver Traffic Guardians and AI Self-Driving Cars

8   Anti-Gridlock Laws and AI Self-Driving Cars

9   Arguing Machines and AI Self-Driving Cars

*This title is available via Amazon and other book sellers*

Companion Book By This Author

***AI Self-Driving Cars***
**Breakthroughs**

by Dr. Lance B. Eliot, MBA, PhD

Chapter Title

1   Eliot Framework for AI Self-Driving Cars

2   Off-Roading and AI Self-Driving Cars

3   Paralleling Vehicles and AI Self-Driving Cars

4   Dementia Drivers and AI Self-Driving Cars

5   Augmented Realty (AR) and AI Self-Driving Cars

6   Sleeping Inside an AI Self-Driving Car

7   Prevalence Detection and AI Self-Driving Cars

8   Super-Intelligent AI and AI Self-Driving Cars

9   Car Caravans and AI Self-Driving Cars

*This title is available via Amazon and other book sellers*

Companion Book By This Author

### *Trailblazing Trends for* **AI Self-Driving Cars**

by Dr. Lance B. Eliot, MBA, PhD

Chapter Title

1  Eliot Framework for AI Self-Driving Cars

2  Strategic AI Metaphors and AI Self-Driving Cars

3  Emergency-Only AI and AI Self-Driving Cars

4  Animal Drawn Vehicles and AI Self-Driving Cars

5  Chess Play and AI Self-Driving Cars

6  Cobots Exoskeletons and AI Self-Driving Car

7  Economic Commodity and AI Self-Driving Cars

8  Road Racing and AI Self-Driving Cars

*This title is available via Amazon and other book sellers*

Companion Book By This Author

### *Ingenious Strides for* **AI Driverless Cars**

by Dr. Lance B. Eliot, MBA, PhD

Chapter Title

1  Eliot Framework for AI Self-Driving Cars

2  Plasticity and AI Self-Driving Cars

3  NIMBY vs. YIMBY and AI Self-Driving Cars

4  Top Trends for 2019 and AI Self-Driving Cars

5  Rural Areas and AI Self-Driving Cars

6  Self-Imposed Constraints and AI Self-Driving Car

7  Alien Limb Syndrome and AI Self-Driving Cars

8  Jaywalking and AI Self-Driving Cars

*This title is available via Amazon and other book sellers*

Companion Book By This Author

### *AI Self-Driving Cars*
### *Inventiveness*

by Dr. Lance B. Eliot, MBA, PhD


Chapter Title

1  Eliot Framework for AI Self-Driving Cars

2  Crumbling Infrastructure and AI Self-Driving Cars

3  e-Billboarding and AI Self-Driving Cars

4  Kinship and AI Self-Driving Cars

5  Machine-Child Learning and AI Self-Driving Cars

6  Baby-on-Board and AI Self-Driving Car

7  Cop Car Chases and AI Self-Driving Cars

8  One-Shot Learning and AI Self-Driving Cars

*This title is available via Amazon and other book sellers*

Companion Book By This Author

### *Visionary Secrets of AI Driverless Cars*

by Dr. Lance B. Eliot, MBA, PhD

Chapter Title

1  Eliot Framework for AI Self-Driving Cars

2  Seat Belts and AI Self-Driving Cars

3  Tiny EV's and AI Self-Driving Cars

4  Empathetic Computing and AI Self-Driving Cars

5  Ethics Global Variations and AI Self-Driving Cars

6  Computational Periscopy and AI Self-Driving Car

7  Superior Cognition and AI Self-Driving Cars

8  Amalgamating ODD's and AI Self-Driving Cars

*This title is available via Amazon and other book sellers*

Companion Book By This Author

### *Spearheading*
### *AI Self-Driving Cars*

by Dr. Lance B. Eliot, MBA, PhD

Chapter Title

1   Eliot Framework for AI Self-Driving Cars

2   Artificial Pain and AI Self-Driving Cars

3   Stop-and-Frisks and AI Self-Driving Cars

4   Cars Careening and AI Self-Driving Cars

5   Sounding Out Car Noises and AI Self-Driving Cars

6   No Speed Limit Autobahn and AI Self-Driving Car

7   Noble Cause Corruption and AI Self-Driving Cars

8   AI Rockstars and AI Self-Driving Cars

*This title is available via Amazon and other book sellers*

Companion Book By This Author

*Spurring*
*AI Self-Driving Cars*

by Dr. Lance B. Eliot, MBA, PhD

Chapter Title

1   Eliot Framework for AI Self-Driving Cars

2   Triune Brain Theory and AI Self-Driving Cars

3   Car Parts Thefts and AI Self-Driving Cars

4   Goto Fail Bug and AI Self-Driving Cars

5   Scrabble Understanding and AI Self-Driving Cars

6   Cognition Disorders and AI Self-Driving Car

7   Noise Pollution Abatement AI Self-Driving Cars

*This title is available via Amazon and other book sellers*

Companion Book By This Author

### *Avant-Garde*
### *AI Driverless Cars*

by Dr. Lance B. Eliot, MBA, PhD

Chapter Title

1  Eliot Framework for AI Self-Driving Cars

2  Linear Non-Threshold and AI Self-Driving Cars

3  Prediction Equation and AI Self-Driving Cars

4  Modular Autonomous Systems and AI Self-Driving Cars

5  Driver's Licensing and AI Self-Driving Cars

6  Offshoots and Spinoffs and AI Self-Driving Car

7  Depersonalization and AI Self-Driving Cars

*This title is available via Amazon and other book sellers*

Companion Book By This Author

## *AI Self-Driving Cars*
## *Evolvement*

by Dr. Lance B. Eliot, MBA, PhD

Chapter Title

1   Eliot Framework for AI Self-Driving Cars

2   Chief Safety Officers and AI Self-Driving Cars

3   Bounded Volumes and AI Self-Driving Cars

4   Micro-Movements Behaviors and AI Self-Driving Cars

5   Boeing 737 Aspects and AI Self-Driving Cars

6   Car Controls Commands and AI Self-Driving Car

7   Multi-Sensor Data Fusion and AI Self-Driving Cars

*This title is available via Amazon and other book sellers*

Companion Book By This Author

### *AI Driverless Cars*
### *Chrysalis*

by Dr. Lance B. Eliot, MBA, PhD

<u>Chapter Title</u>

1  Eliot Framework for AI Self-Driving Cars

2  Object Poses and AI Self-Driving Cars

3  Human In-The-Loop and AI Self-Driving Cars

4  Genius Shortage and AI Self-Driving Cars

5  Salvage Yards and AI Self-Driving Cars

6  Precision Scheduling and AI Self-Driving Car

7  Human Driving Extinction and AI Self-Driving Cars

*This title is available via Amazon and other book sellers*

Companion Book By This Author

*Boosting*
*AI Autonomous Cars*

by Dr. Lance B. Eliot, MBA, PhD

Chapter Title

1   Eliot Framework for AI Self-Driving Cars

2   Zero Knowledge Proofs and AI Self-Driving Cars

3   Active Shooter Response and AI Self-Driving Cars

4   Free Will and AI Self-Driving Cars

5   No Picture Yet of AI Self-Driving Cars

6   Boeing 737 Lessons and AI Self-Driving Cars

7   Preview Tesla FSD and AI Self-Driving Cars

8   LIDAR Industry and AI Self-Driving Cars

9   Uber IPO and AI Self-Driving Cars

10   Suing Automakers of AI Self-Driving Cars

11   Tesla Overarching FSD and AI Self-Driving Cars

12   Auto Repair Market and AI Self-Driving Cars

*This title is available via Amazon and other book sellers*

Companion Book By This Author

## *AI Self-Driving Cars Trendsetting*

by Dr. Lance B. Eliot, MBA, PhD

Chapter Title

1  Eliot Framework for AI Self-Driving Cars

2  OTA Myths and AI Self-Driving Cars

3  Surveys and AI Self-Driving Cars

4  Tech Spies and AI Self-Driving Cars

5  Anxieties and AI Self-Driving Cars

6  Achilles Heel and AI Self-Driving Cars

7  Kids Alone and AI Self-Driving Cars

8  Infrastructure and AI Self-Driving Cars

9  Distracted Driving and AI Self-Driving Cars

10  Human Drivers and AI Self-Driving Cars

11  Anti-LIDAR Stance and AI Self-Driving Cars

12  Autopilot Team and AI Self-Driving Cars

13  Rigged Videos and AI Self-Driving Cars

14  Stalled Cars and AI Self-Driving Cars

15  Princeton Summit and AI Self-Driving Cars

16  Brittleness and AI Self-Driving Cars

17  Mergers and AI Self-Driving Cars

*This title is available via Amazon and other book sellers*

Companion Book By This Author

### *AI Autonomous Cars*
### *Forefront*

by Dr. Lance B. Eliot, MBA, PhD

Chapter Title

1  Eliot Framework for AI Self-Driving Cars

2  Essential Stats and AI Self-Driving Cars

3  Stats Fallacies and AI Self-Driving Cars

4  Driver Bullies and AI Self-Driving Cars

5  Sunday Drives and AI Self-Driving Cars

6  Face Recog Bans and AI Self-Driving Cars

7  States On-The-Hook and AI Self-Driving Cars

8  Sensors Profiting and AI Self-Driving Cars

9  Unruly Riders and AI Self-Driving Cars

10  Father's Day and AI Self-Driving Cars

11  Summons Feature and AI Self-Driving Cars

12  Libra Cryptocurrency and AI Self-Driving Cars

13  Systems Naming and AI Self-Driving Cars

14  Mid-Traffic Rendezvous and AI Self-Driving Cars

15  Pairing Drones and AI Self-Driving Cars

16  Lost Wallet Study and AI Self-Driving Cars

*This title is available via Amazon and other book sellers*

Companion Book By This Author

## *AI Autonomous Cars Emergence*

by Dr. Lance B. Eliot, MBA, PhD

Chapter Title

1   Eliot Framework for AI Self-Driving Cars

2   Dropping Off Riders and AI Self-Driving Cars

3   Add-On Kits Drive.AI and AI Self-Driving Cars

4   Boeing 737 Emergency Flaw and AI Self-Driving Cars

5   Spinout Tesla Autopilot and AI Self-Driving Cars

6   Earthquakes and AI Self-Driving Cars

7   Ford Mobility Lab and AI Self-Driving Cars

8   Apollo 11 Error Code and AI Self-Driving Cars

9   Nuro Self-Driving Vehicle and AI Self-Driving Cars

10   Safety First (SaFAD) Aptiv and AI Self-Driving Cars

11   Brainjacking Neuralink and AI Self-Driving Cars

12   Storming Area 51 and AI Self-Driving Cars

13   Riding Inside An AI Self-Driving Car

14   ACES Acronym and AI Self-Driving Cars

15   Kids Bike Riding and AI Self-Driving Cars

16   LIDAR Not Doomed and AI Self-Driving Cars

*This title is available via Amazon and other book sellers*

Companion Book By This Author

## *AI Autonomous Cars Progress*

by Dr. Lance B. Eliot, MBA, PhD

Chapter Title

1   Eliot Framework for AI Self-Driving Cars

2   Risk-O-Meters and AI Self-Driving Cars

3   Eroding Car Devotion and AI Self-Driving Cars

4   Drunk Driving Rises With Smart Cars

5   Driver's Difficulties and Smart Cars

6   Millennials Aren't As Car Crazed As Baby Boomers

7   Risks Of AI Self-Driving Cars

8   Major Phase Shift and AI Self-Driving Cars

9   Level 3 Tech Misgivings For Smart Cars

10   Presidential Debate Lessons and AI Self-Driving Cars

11   Cloud Breeches and AI Self-Driving Cars

12   The Moral Imperative and AI Self-Driving Cars

13   Freed Up Driver Time And AI Self-Driving Car

14   Deadliest Highways and AI Self-Driving Cars

15   Your Lyin' Eyes and AI Self-Driving Cars

16   Elon Musk Physics Mindset and AI Self-Driving Cars

**This title is available via Amazon and other book sellers**

## *AI Self-Driving Cars Prognosis*

by Dr. Lance B. Eliot, MBA, PhD

Chapter Title

1   Eliot Framework for AI Self-Driving Cars

2   Roadkill and AI Self-Driving Cars

3   Safe Driver Cities and AI Self-Driving Cars

4   Tailgate Parties and AI Self-Driving Cars

5   Tesla's AI Chips and AI Self-Driving Cars

6   Elites-Only and AI Self-Driving Cars

7   Four Year Lifecycle and AI Self-Driving Cars

8   Entrepreneurs and AI Self-Driving Cars

9   Autopilot Crash Lessons and AI Self-Driving Cars

10   U.N. Framework and AI Self-Driving Cars

11   Sports Cars and AI Self-Driving Cars

12   Railroad Crossings and AI Self-Driving Cars

13   Robots That Drive and AI Self-Driving Car

14   Smarts Over Speed and AI Self-Driving Cars

15   Havoc Ratings and AI Self-Driving Cars

16   Sex-on-Wheels and AI Self-Driving Cars

*This title is available via Amazon and other book sellers*

Companion Book By This Author

## *AI Self-Driving Cars Momentum*

by Dr. Lance B. Eliot, MBA, PhD

Chapter Title

1  Eliot Framework for AI Self-Driving Cars

2  Solving Loneliness and AI Self-Driving Cars

3  Headless Issues and AI Self-Driving Cars

4  Roaming Empty and AI Self-Driving Cars

5  Millennials Exodus and AI Self-Driving Cars

6  Recession Worries and AI Self-Driving Cars

7  Remote Operation Issues and AI Self-Driving Cars

8  Boomerang Kids and AI Self-Driving Cars

9  Waymo Coming To L.A. and AI Self-Driving Cars

10  Getting To Scale and AI Self-Driving Cars

11  Looking Alike and AI Self-Driving Cars

12  NOVA Documentary On AI Self-Driving Cars

13  Birthrate Changes and AI Self-Driving Cars

*This title is available via Amazon and other book sellers*

<u>Companion Book By This Author</u>

## *AI Self-Driving Cars*
## *Headway*

by Dr. Lance B. Eliot, MBA, PhD

<u>Chapter Title</u>

1   Eliot Framework for AI Self-Driving Cars

2   Germs Spreading and AI Self-Driving Cars

3   Carbon Footprint and AI Self-Driving Cars

4   Protestors Use Of AI Self-Driving Cars

5   Rogue Behavior and AI Self-Driving Cars

6   Using Human Drivers Versus AI Self-Driving Cars

7   Tesla Hodge-Podge On AI Self-Driving Cars

8   Solo Occupancy and AI Self-Driving Cars

9   Einstein's Twins Paradox and AI Self-Driving Cars

10   Nation-State Takeover Of AI Self-Driving Cars

11   Quantum Computers and AI Self-Driving Cars

12   Religious Revival And AI Self-Driving Cars

*This title is available via Amazon and other book sellers*

# ABOUT THE AUTHOR

Dr. Lance B. Eliot, MBA, PhD is the CEO of Techbruim, Inc. and Executive Director of the Cybernetic AI Self-Driving Car Institute and has over twenty years of industry experience including serving as a corporate officer in a billion dollar firm and was a partner in a major executive services firm. He is also a serial entrepreneur having founded, ran, and sold several high-tech related businesses. He previously hosted the popular radio show *Technotrends* that was also available on American Airlines flights via their in-flight audio program. Author or co-author of a dozen books and over 400 articles, he has made appearances on CNN, and has been a frequent speaker at industry conferences.

A former professor at the University of Southern California (USC), he founded and led an innovative research lab on Artificial Intelligence in Business. Known as the "AI Insider" his writings on AI advances and trends has been widely read and cited. He also previously served on the faculty of the University of California Los Angeles (UCLA), and was a visiting professor at other major universities. He was elected to the International Board of the Society for Information Management (SIM), a prestigious association of over 3,000 high-tech executives worldwide.

He has performed extensive community service, including serving as Senior Science Adviser to the Vice Chair of the Congressional Committee on Science & Technology. He has served on the Board of the OC Science & Engineering Fair (OCSEF), where he is also has been a Grand Sweepstakes judge, and likewise served as a judge for the Intel International SEF (ISEF). He served as the Vice Chair of the Association for Computing Machinery (ACM) Chapter, a prestigious association of computer scientists. Dr. Eliot has been a shark tank judge for the USC Mark Stevens Center for Innovation on start-up pitch competitions, and served as a mentor for several incubators and accelerators in Silicon Valley and Silicon Beach. He served on several Boards and Committees at USC, including having served on the Marshall Alumni Association (MAA) Board in Southern California.

Dr. Eliot holds a PhD from USC, MBA, and Bachelor's in Computer Science, and earned the CDP, CCP, CSP, CDE, and CISA certifications. Born and raised in Southern California, and having traveled and lived internationally, he enjoys scuba diving, surfing, and sailing.

# ADDENDUM

## *AI Self-Driving Cars Headway*

*Practical Advances in Artificial Intelligence (AI) and Machine Learning*

By
Dr. Lance B. Eliot, MBA, PhD

———

For supplemental materials of this book, visit:
**www.ai-selfdriving-cars.guru**

For special orders of this book, contact:
**LBE Press Publishing**
Email: LBE.Press.Publishing@gmail.com

www.ingramcontent.com/pod-product-compliance
Lightning Source LLC
Chambersburg PA
CBHW051048050326
40690CB00006B/638